This book bel

D0287448

The
HEART
of
faith

A FIELD GUIDE FOR
CATECHUMENS
& CANDIDATES

Nick Wagner

TWENTY
THIRD 23rd
PUBLICATIONS

TWENTY-THIRD PUBLICATIONS
A Division of Bayard
One Montauk Avenue, Suite 200
New London, CT 06320
(860) 437-3012 or (800) 321-0411
www.23rdpublications.com

The Scripture passages contained herein are from the *New Revised Standard Version of the Bible*, copyright ©1989, by the Division of Christian Education of the National Council of Churches in the U.S.A. All rights reserved.

ISBN 978-1-58595-817-7
Library of Congress Control Number: 2010938682
Printed in the U.S.A.

Contents

How to use this book

This book is for all those who are preparing to become Catholic. I think Catholics see the world differently from most folks—even differently from some other Christians. This book is meant to be a guide to help you understand that difference.

I would suggest you read through the first four chapters (Introduction, Living the Jesus way, Imagine seeing God, and See the world with Catholic eyes). Then take a break. Reflect on what you read. (There are questions at the end of the chapters that will help you with that.) Perhaps even go back and re-read sections that interested you.

Then, it's up to you how you might read the rest of the book. If you're like me, you can't wait to get to the end of a book. So you may want to read the rest straight through. Another way to read the book is to pick and choose. What's going on in your formation process right now? Perhaps you want to leaf through the book to find the section that speaks to what you are learning at this moment. If you are interested in some of the nuts-and-bolts aspects of being Catholic, turn to the appendices for some quick descriptions and definitions. There is no one right way to use this resource. Adapt it to what works best for your situation.

Here is an important thing to understand, however. This is not a textbook of the faith. It's not supposed to replace or substitute for the formation process in your parish. In your parish, you should be meeting regularly to break open God's word, explore the teaching of the church, and practice participating in the mission of the church. Your parish leaders will help you learn how to do those things.

This is more of a lifestyle book. If you've ever wondered "why Catholics do that," this book will help you understand the spirituality and outlook behind the way we live in the world. And my prayer for you is that this book will help you be a better Catholic.

Blessings on your journey.

Important dates
on your journey of faith

Some of the dates below are fixed and some change every year. Ask someone from your initiation team to help you fill in the variable dates.

First Sunday of Advent   _____

Solemnity of the Immaculate Conception   December 8

Christmas   December 25

Epiphany   _____

Solemnity of Mary, Mother of God   January 1

Ash Wednesday   _____

First Sunday of Lent / Rite of Election   _____

Second Sunday of Lent
(optional penitential rite)   _____

Third Sunday of Lent / First scrutiny   _____

Presentation of the Creed   _____

Fourth Sunday of Lent / Second scrutiny _____

Fifth Sunday of Lent / Third scrutiny _____

Presentation of the Lord's Prayer _____

Palm Sunday _____

Holy Thursday _____

Good Friday _____

Holy Saturday / Preparation Rites /
    Easter Vigil _____

Easter Sunday _____

Neophyte Mass _____

Solemnity of the Ascension _____

Pentecost _____

Solemnity of the Assumption of Mary   August 15

All Saints Day   November 1

Rite of Acceptance
    into the Order of Catechumens _____

Rite of Welcoming the Candidates _____

Introduction

"HOW DO I BECOME A CATHOLIC?"

There was a long pause as I tried to form an answer. I had gotten the call because I was the only staff person in the parish office that day. I was twenty-six, and this was early in my first job in parish ministry. I knew the parish had an RCIA program, but I didn't know who the contact person was, when the group met, or how to direct the caller to her next step.

And I was remembering when I had a similar question myself. I've been Catholic all my life, but I haven't always known how to *be* Catholic. I went to a Catholic elementary school, and I went to Mass every day with my classmates. We had religion class every day, and I was taught by both nuns and dedicated Catholic lay women who took seriously their mission to educate me in the faith. Even so, when I started ninth grade in a public high school, I thought I was done with "learning" about religion. I still went to Mass every Sunday, but mostly because my mother expected it.

After a while, however, some of my classmates tried to "evangelize" me. I don't think they knew I was Catholic. I don't think it would have mattered if they did. These kids believed they had a mission. I'd find out later that their mission was to make sure everybody they met had a chance to know who Jesus is and know that Jesus loves them.

✚ Evangelization by hanging out ✚

They were pretty gentle, as Southern evangelicals go. They didn't try to scare me with stories of eternal damnation, and they didn't throw a lot of Bible verses at me. They just invited me to hang out with them.

What struck me about them, though, was how easily and freely they talked about Jesus. And they would pray about *everything*. All the time. Anywhere, for any reason. If we were trying to decide what movie to see, someone would say, "Let's pray about it." If it rained, they'd say a prayer thanking God for the rain. If we went to one of our school's football games, they'd pray for our team *and the other team!*

As a good Catholic, I knew how to pray. But gosh, there's a time and a place for everything. Prayer was something that was scheduled for certain times of the day or week. As far as I knew, the only time Catholics prayed outside the lines was in case of an emergency.

There was something else about the way my evangelical friends prayed that was different. They prayed in a way that seemed they were talking to someone they knew really well—someone they were really close to. When I prayed, it was more like mailing a very formal letter to the president of a large corporation.

✚ The power of prayer ✚

And my friends prayed with such confidence—as though they had some special access to a room where prayers from important people landed. Years later, I heard a story that reminded me of my friends. One summer, a small farming community was suffering terribly from an unending drought. They turned to their pastor and begged him to tell them what to do. Being a good pastor, he decided everyone needed to pray more. In fact, he scheduled an extra service for the following Sunday, just to pray for rain. He told all of his flock to spread the word. Go out, and gather everyone you can find, he said. He set out to send up a prayer to beat all prayers next Sunday.

Everyone was busy all week getting ready. They planned music and chose special readings from the Bible. They wrote prayers and petitions and pleadings to the Almighty. They planned a celebration supper to be held after the prayer. They invited the mayor, the fire marshal, and the police chief.

Then the moment of prayer arrived. The whole town turned out. People were dressed in their finest Sunday clothes, shoes shined, shirts pressed, dresses primped, hair sprayed. It was a fine and colorful procession of the Christian faithful.

And at the very end of the procession was a little girl, not dressed like the others. She, alone, wore a raincoat and carried an umbrella.

My friends were the little girl, all the time. I was the rest of the town that wasn't all that confident in my prayer being answered.

When I prayed, I knew the prayer got delivered. But I was never quite sure how much time the Boss had to hear it or respond to it. God's a pretty busy deity, after all. Often I'd direct my prayer to a saint who was in charge of whatever category my prayer fell into. Or, if I wanted to be extra sure my prayer got answered, I'd pray to Mary.

The thing that impressed me most about my friends was the way they lived every minute of their lives as though their faith mattered to them. It's not that my faith didn't matter to me, but it was a few levels down. It certainly wasn't something I talked about in public. It was handy to have when someone was sick or I had a big test coming up. But it wasn't something I thought about most days.

✦ Heaven is now ✦

So, it was about ten years later when someone called my parish and asked me how to become Catholic. I wanted to ask, "Do you mean Catholic like I used to be, or Catholic like I learned to be?"

What I learned in those ten years is that I was absent from class a lot of the time in Catholic grade school. I was physically present, but the message didn't get through. I thought being a good Catholic meant keeping the rules. If I learned what the rules were and kept to them, I'd get to go to heaven when I died. And for a long time, I really thought that's what it was all about.

What I learned from my evangelical friends was that heaven is now! All the promises, all the grace, all the love, all the peace—all of it is in our hearts right now. I learned that being Catholic isn't all about keeping the rules. It is about—to borrow a phrase from my high school friends—keeping the faith.

Now don't get me wrong. Being Catholic is not a do-it-yourself project. There are rules, to be sure. But the rules don't exist for the sake of rules. They exist for the same reason music has meter. Or baseball has foul lines. Or writing has grammar. The form of the thing provides a structure within which to do something beautiful.

✢ The heart of becoming Catholic ✢

My caller was still waiting to find out what she had to do to become Catholic. I wanted to tell her, just do what Catholics do. But I knew she could hear that in two different ways, as I had. She could hear that as "learn and follow the rules." And I wanted her to hear it as something deeper. I wanted to tell her how to become Catholic in her heart.

To become Catholic, you have to have a change of heart. Becoming Catholic is a process of falling in love. The person we're falling in love with, over and over again, more and more deeply, is Jesus Christ. To become Catholic, you have to open your heart to the love Jesus has for you and return that love as best you can. If you've ever loved a child, a spouse, an aging parent, a sibling, a best friend—you know that "love" is not always an easy job. Loving Jesus means all that. And it also means loving the stranger, and the person who doesn't deserve it, and even our enemy. Loving our loved ones is hard enough. Loving our unloved ones can seem impossible. And yet, that's how you become Catholic.

The day I figured *that* out, I was asking God if maybe, please, could I just go back to being a good little rule-keeping Catholic. You can guess what the answer was.

So, my poor caller is still there, patiently waiting on the line. How could I tell her all that? How could I possibly say in a brief phone conversation what she needed to do to become Catholic? Honestly, I don't remember exactly what I told her. It was probably some version of what my high school evangelists had said to me: "Just come hang out with us for a while."

But I do want to try to tell you what you need to do to become Catholic. Not so much about the rules. Someone on your parish initiation team will cover all that with you. I want to talk more about the heart of what it means to become Catholic. And that's what the rest of this book is about.

✢ Catholic or Christian? ✢

Before we get started, we have to do a little sorting of seekers. When Catholics talk about being Catholic, we mean "Christian." So why don't we just say that? Honestly, I don't know. Some people refer to soft drinks as "pop," and others say "soda." It's just the way most Catholics talk.

So being Catholic is the same thing as being Christian. Is being Christian the same thing as being Catholic? No, not always. Throughout the centuries, there have been groups that have split off from the Catholic Church because they saw things differently. Even though some groups of Christians have different views than others, the one view we all share is that we see God through the eyes of Jesus, and we see the world through the eyes of Jesus.

So if you are already a Christian who is thinking of becoming Roman Catholic, your journey could be very different from someone who is not Christian. In some ways, the shift from another form of Christianity to Catholicism isn't as life-changing as it is for someone who has never seen Jesus. Now, if you've been Christian in name only all your life, perhaps you've never really met Jesus either. If that's the case, your journey might be more like the non-Christian's.

As we look at how living the Catholic (Christian) way will transform your life, keep in mind that we are talking about three different kinds of folks (with lots of individual exceptions):

1. unbaptized folks

2. baptized, non-practicing folks

3. baptized folks

The path is a little different for each group. As we go through the book together, I'll point out where the path branches off for the different groups.

✦ Who is Jesus? ✦

I talked earlier about being in love with Jesus. If you are baptized, you know what I'm talking about. If you are unbaptized or baptized, non-practicing, you might not know what I mean. Folks who are not Christian (and even some Christians) tend to think of Jesus as a historical figure, like George Washington or Gandhi. We don't imagine we will ever see George Washington or meet Gandhi. While Jesus was a historical figure, that's not how most Christians think of him. We believe Jesus died and that he is no longer dead. We believe Jesus was raised from the dead. We believe Jesus is alive in heaven and alive in the church on earth. And we believe Jesus is coming in glory at the end of time.

When I talk about falling in love with Jesus and having a change of heart, I'm talking about transforming your life. I'm talking about transforming your life to live the way Jesus did. So before you can think of joining the Catholic Church, you have to think of joining Jesus. For me, it's one and the same thing. But it didn't used to be. And some of the folks I've met along the way thought they were joining an institution and didn't fully understand they were joining a person.

- If you are baptized, describe what you remember about your baptism. If you are not baptized, describe a baptism you may have witnessed or what you think happens at baptism.

- We talked about how baptism is more about joining a person than joining an institution. How would you describe this difference?

- Why do you want to become a Catholic?

- Who is Jesus for you?

Living the Jesus way

WE ARE NOT THE FIRST GENERATION to struggle with learning to live in relationship with Jesus. About sixty to seventy years after Jesus' death, John, one of Jesus' disciples, wrote down the story of Jesus' life, death, and resurrection. But John's story was not a simple biography. It was a template or a guidebook for living life in a new way—the Jesus way.

Gospel

You're going to hear the word "gospel" a lot in your preparation process. The word has a lot of different meanings. It comes from the Greek word **evangelion**—*from which we also get "evangelization." The broadest meaning of gospel is "good news." The good news, or the gospel, is everything that Jesus told us and taught us.*

Gospel can also refer to one of the four books in the Bible that tell the story of Jesus. These books were written by disciples (followers) of Jesus. The authors' names are Matthew, Mark, Luke, and John.

Finally, we refer to the gospel in the Mass. In the first part of the Mass, called the liturgy of the word, we hear two or three readings. The final reading is always a passage from one of the four gospels in the Bible. Catholics believe that Jesus is present and is speaking to us in the word proclaimed at Mass and that the gospel is the high point of the liturgy of the word.

✴ How to read the stories about Jesus ✴

John's story is not written in the style of modern self-help books, however. Nor is it meant to be read like a history book. It is written in a way that stimulates our imaginations. John's story has multiple layers of meaning, and it requires us to use our imaginations actively to get the full impact of what he wants to tell us.

When I first encountered John's story, some of the symbolism he used confused me. I read a little about what his symbolism might mean, and then the story began to make more sense. But I also wondered why he didn't just speak clearly in the first place. Why bother with all those confusing symbols?

Eventually, I came to understand that John didn't mean just one thing. He also meant another thing, and another, and something else besides. Painters and poets can't say just one thing because what they are trying to describe cannot be said only one way. They have to use images, symbols, and metaphors to communicate the deep mystery of what they see in life. John and many of the other writers in the Bible are the same way. They are saying many things at once, and they use artistic tools to communicate the mystery of the person of Jesus.

Let's look at an example. In John's gospel, there is a story about Jesus feeding a large crowd of hungry people.

John 6:1–15

Jesus went across the Sea of Galilee. A large crowd followed him, because they saw the signs he was performing on the sick. Jesus went up on the mountain, and there he sat down with his disciples. The Jewish feast of Passover was near. When Jesus raised his eyes and saw that a large crowd was coming to him, he said to Philip, "Where can we buy enough food for them to eat?" He said this to test him, because he himself knew what he was going to do. Philip answered him, "Two hundred days' wages worth of food would not be enough for each of them to have a little." One of his disciples, Andrew, the brother of Simon Peter, said to him, "There is a boy here who has five

barley loaves and two fish; but what good are these for so many?"
Jesus said, "Have the people recline." Now there was a great deal
of grass in that place. So the men reclined, about five thousand in
number. Then Jesus took the loaves, gave thanks, and distributed
them to those who were reclining, and also as much of the fish as
they wanted. When they had had their fill, he said to his disciples,
"Gather the fragments left over, so that nothing will be wasted." So
they collected them, and filled twelve wicker baskets with fragments
from the five barley loaves that had been more than they could eat.
When the people saw the sign he had done, they said, "This is truly
the Prophet, the one who is to come into the world." Since Jesus knew
that they were going to come and carry him off to make him king, he
withdrew again to the mountain alone.

You can tell right away this isn't just a story about food service. Look at his dialogue with Philip. John tells us that Jesus is testing Philip with his question. If we are reading the story literally, we might think Jesus is being a little tough on Philip, and we might be relieved that we aren't Philip. But we are! That's one of the points John is trying to make. Philip, one of Jesus' disciples, is also a symbol for all of Jesus' disciples. Philip's response sets up one possible way of looking at the situation before them.

Philip's reply indicates the situation seems hopeless. There is no way to feed all these people. Our resources are very scarce, and the demand is very large. It would be better to just send the people away because the situation is impossible.

Andrew, another disciple, backs up Philip's assessment. He's discovered a boy who has a little bit of food, but it's not nearly enough.

Use your imagination here, and try to see what Jesus is seeing. Hungry crowd, reluctant, discouraged disciples, and a boy offering whatever resources he has, however inadequate they might be. The logical thing to do, the safe thing to do, would be to send the people away. Jesus' response is not logical. He directs the disciples to have people recline on the grass.

In ancient Jewish culture, reclining was the posture for eating. So Jesus has set up a bit of a dangerous expectation here. He has told the disciples to get the people ready for a meal, even though it's clear he has no possible means of feeding them.

At this point in the story, John increases the dramatic tension. So far, we only know the crowd is "large." He then whacks us on the head with the exact number—5,000 men! Impossibly large! And yet somehow, he pulls it off. Not only does he feed the massive crowd, there are baskets and baskets of leftovers.

Jesus has completely upended the assessment of his disciples. Where they saw scarcity, he saw abundance. When they were hopeless, he showed crazy hopefulness. What they saw as an impossible situation, Jesus saw as a banquet of God's love.

How was Jesus able to see the world so differently than his disciples did? How was Jesus able to provide for an impossibly large number of people in the face of seemingly overwhelming obstacles? We have to use our imaginations again and look at the symbols John is using in the story.

Look at where the food came from. In most ancient cultures, children and women were not held in high esteem. Note that in the story, only the number of men is recorded. It would not have been important to identify how many women and children were also present. And yet, the food for the crowd came from a child. While the disciples are quick to dismiss the offerings of the insignificant one as inadequate, Jesus does not. He immediately recognizes the great sacrifice the child is making and pays attention to it. He gives thanks for it.

If Philip and Andrew are symbols of the disciples, the child is a symbol of those Jesus came to pay attention to. He is a symbol of all those the world sees as insignificant and inadequate. Jesus does not pay attention to the insiders. He pays attention to the outsider. The insiders believe we live in a world of scarcity. The outsider believes we have enough to share with everyone—and baskets left over.

There are more symbols to pay attention to. The 5,000 are a symbol of all humanity. Jesus sets them down on the place of creation—God's green earth. He is about to recreate their world. He is going to transform their lives. He participates in a new creation in which no one is ever hungry again. And the child, the outsider, is a co-creator with him. The radical generosity of the child is a creative act that establishes a new reality. Where once we saw scarcity and barrenness, now we see life and abundant resources.

Finally, there is one more level to this story. John never tells us *specifically* how five loaves and a couple of fish became a feast for the masses. He only tells us which response Jesus paid attention to. When faced with the needs of the world, Jesus ignored the response of the insiders (the scarcity response) and paid attention to the response of the outsider (the generosity response). Then he leaves us to draw the conclusion for our own lives. Do we see the world as a place of scarce resources or as a new creation? When we meet others in need, will we hoard what we have and tell them to go away? Or will we invite them to stay and offer everything we have out of radical generosity? Will we align ourselves with the safety of the insiders or risk everything by embracing the outsider?

Every gospel story is really asking questions like these. And everything we do as disciples of Jesus indicates what our answer is. For those of us who are baptized, we believe in the new creation in which the world is a place of abundance. Each day, we try to get a little better, practicing more and more to offer what we have to give, believing it will be more than enough. Even so, we often act like Philip and Andrew and revert to our old ways of planning for scarcity.

For the unbaptized and the non-practicing baptized, you may not yet completely believe in the new creation. That is part of the journey of faith. The job of the believers is to show by example what it means to live in faith that there will always be more than enough. Your job is to try to imitate us (as we try to imitate Christ) and grow stronger every day until you come to a point where you believe, also.

(I am grateful to my pastor, Fr. Jon Pedigo, for a Sunday homily he preached that inspired this reflection on the feeding of the 5,000.)

✣ Are you on the right path? ✣

In 1521, Íñigo López de Loyola was a successful soldier in the Spanish army. He had been baptized as a child and had grown up Catholic. From all outward appearances, he seemed to be on the right path. But he had never really grown to love Jesus. He had a spiritual emptiness. Then, on May 20 of that year, he was badly wounded in both legs. He underwent several painful operations and spent a long time recovering. During that time, he read about the life of Jesus and the lives of many of the saints. He became passionate about wanting to imitate the saintly heroes he read about. After he could walk again, he gave up his military life and devoted himself to evangelizing those who didn't know about Jesus.

After that time, he was known as Ignatius, and he became as heroic as the saints he sought to imitate. He founded the Society of Jesus (the Jesuits), and developed a method of spiritual practice that is still used today. He was canonized as a saint on March 13, 1622, and we celebrate his feast day on July 31.

In his teachings about spirituality, Ignatius says we must discern between good spirits and bad spirits if we are to know how to truly follow Jesus. You may have noticed an internal struggle within yourself that mirrors Ignatius' teaching. You may have gotten this far in your life without paying much attention to God or to your spiritual life. But something is now drawing you to Jesus. Some of your previous lifestyle may be compatible with a Christian way of life and some may not. The spirit of your old life and the spirit of Jesus may both be attractive to you, and you will have to discern which to choose—which will lead to your happiness.

For some people, the choice is clear. And for others, it's a difficult choice. Some people choose, change their minds, and then change their minds again. And it's not just the unbaptized folks who need to discern the correct path. Even the saints among us struggle with trying to know God's will and live as Christ would have us live. We get tempted and think perhaps there is something better out there that we are missing.

This sense of being attracted to conflicting lifestyles or values can seem confusing. What you'll hear some people say (heck, what you'll hear me say) is that it is difficult to know what God wants us to do.

Is God's will for us really that unclear? Well, no, not really. It's like the mountain climber who slipped and almost fell to his death. At the last minute, he was able to grab the limb of a tree growing off the side of the mountain. As he dangled about 900 feet above the canyon floor, he shouted to God to save him. God replied in a booming voice, "Fear not. I will save you."

"Thank you, Lord!" replied the man. "Can you really save me?"

"Yes," boomed the Lord. "Let go of the branch."

"What?!?!?" yelled the man. "Are you crazy?"

"Have faith, my son. Let go, and I will catch you."

There was a long silence. Finally the man said, "Uh...is there anybody else up there I can talk to?"

✴ Discerning God's will for us ✴

Usually we know what we should do. We're just afraid or unwilling. I remember when I was a teenager and had a curfew. If I was out with my friends, having a great time, shouldn't that count for something? Wouldn't my mother want me to be happy? What to do, what to do, I would wonder. Of course I knew what I *should* do. I just didn't feel like doing it.

God isn't hiding. God is all around, in plain sight, guiding us toward the path we should take. What we have to do is start paying attention and having a little faith.

When we start paying attention to the presence of God, things happen. We become more peaceful. We become happier. We are more joyful. Most of all, we are more loving. We realize God loves us—not just a little, but like a crazy moonstruck teenager. And we start loving God right back. Which leads us to realize God is in everyone around us. So we start loving them too. And then everything around us just seems better. Life seems right. And whatever it was that was attractive about a former way of life or a path that would lead us away from Jesus loses its luster.

I am not saying life is never difficult for Christians. Life is difficult for everybody. The difference between a Christian way and a non-Christian way is that Christians are always aware of God's unbounded love, and that gives us hope, no matter how dire things may seem. We know there is always salvation and peace.

What would it be like to be so filled with God's presence, every moment of every day, that we always feel complete peace and total love? I have moments like that, sometimes even hours. I'm still working on "days." I'm not sure I'll ever get to "every day." The reason I don't experience the fullness of God's presence more often is that I get distracted. I stop paying attention. I stop seeing and hearing and feeling God all around me because I get busy with *very important things*. But I'm better now than I used to be. I don't take myself as seriously as I used to. I pay attention more. I practice staying in touch with what's going on inside of me and discerning good spirits from bad.

Most of what you'll be doing in the catechumenate is learning how to pay attention. You'll learn the disciplines that ordinary Catholics practice that help us stay in touch. It isn't brain surgery. Most of us don't have esoteric techniques that require years of monastic asceticism. As I've been saying, seeing God is mostly a matter of paying attention. And the first step in paying attention is knowing what to look for. That's what I want to talk about next.

- Do you see the world primarily as a place of abundance or a place of scarcity? Why?

- When have you felt called by God? What do you think God wants you to do in your life right now?

- When have you ever felt completely filled up by God? When have you felt empty?

- Do you have a favorite saint? What is it about that saint that helps you live a Christian life?

Imagine seeing God

NO ONE KNOWS WHAT GOD LOOKS LIKE. At least that's what one kindergarten teacher thought. She was observing one of her students who was diligently drawing at her table. "I'm drawing God," said the little girl.

"Honey, no one knows what God looks like," said the teacher.

Without pausing or looking up, the girl replied, "They will in a minute."

Well, assuming you don't have a pipeline quite as direct as the girl in the story, what would you say if I asked you to describe God? Suppose I described to you my image of God. If my image differed from yours, which of us would be right? We'd both be right. And we'd both be wrong. God is a mystery, and the only way we can know God is through our imagination. Based on what others have told me and my own experiences, I have images of God that I rely on to tell me who God is.

As Christians, we rely on what Jesus told us and our experience of Jesus to tell us who God is. The images we have of God are given to us by Jesus. Jesus said, "Whoever has seen me has seen the Father" (John 14:9). So for Christians to "see" God, all we have to do is look at Jesus.

✦ The ways we see Jesus ✦

How do we go about seeing Jesus? We don't have video recordings or pictures. So we still have to rely on our imaginations. The imagery we use, however, isn't fantasy or speculation. The story of Jesus, the image of Jesus, has been handed down from generation to generation to our own time. So we have the tradition of the church and the stories of Scripture to tell us who Jesus is—and therefore who God is.

We also have the church community itself. Jesus said, wherever two or three are gathered, he is there with us (see Matthew 18:20). So our experience of the church, the community of Jesus, tells us who Jesus is.

And we have our experience with the poor. It is part of our ancient knowledge that Jesus is present most of all in the least among us—like the boy with the loaves and fish. When we help a stranger, feed someone who is hungry, comfort someone who is sick or grieving, or visit someone who is lonely or in prison, we are doing those things for Jesus.

> *When the Son of Man comes in his glory, and all the angels with him, then he will sit on the throne of his glory. All the nations will be gathered before him, and he will separate people one from another as a shepherd separates the sheep from the goats, and he will put the sheep at his right hand and the goats at the left.*
>
> *Then the king will say to those at his right hand, "Come, you that are blessed by my Father, inherit the kingdom prepared for you from the foundation of the world; for I was hungry and you gave me food, I was thirsty and you gave me something to drink, I was a stranger and you welcomed me, I was naked and you gave me clothing, I was sick and you took care of me, I was in prison and you visited me."*
>
> *Then the righteous will answer him, "Lord, when was it that we saw you hungry and gave you food, or thirsty and gave you something to drink? And when was it that we saw you a stranger and welcomed you, or naked and gave you clothing? And when was it that we saw you sick or in prison and visited you?"*
>
> *And the king will answer them, "Truly I tell you, just as you did it to one of the least of these who are members of my family, you did it to me."*

> *Then he will say to those at his left hand, "You that are accursed, depart from me into the eternal fire prepared for the devil and his angels; for I was hungry and you gave me no food, I was thirsty and you gave me nothing to drink, I was a stranger and you did not welcome me, naked and you did not give me clothing, sick and in prison and you did not visit me."*
>
> *Then they also will answer, "Lord, when was it that we saw you hungry or thirsty or a stranger or naked or sick or in prison, and did not take care of you?"*
>
> *Then he will answer them, "Truly I tell you, just as you did not do it to one of the least of these, you did not do it to me." And these will go away into eternal punishment, but the righteous into eternal life. (Matthew 25:31–46)*

Finally, we have the liturgy, the prayer of the church, to show us who Jesus is. This is our number-one way of knowing Jesus. We say that when the church gathers for worship, it is Christ who worships.

A lot of people who want to become Catholic first of all want to know what they have to know. There are some important things to know. But more important is to learn how to see. Catholics look at the world differently from other people. We see Jesus—and therefore God—in everything. In order to see Jesus in everything, we have to work at developing our imagination. The liturgy is our training camp to help us develop our religious imaginations and become more attuned to the presence of Jesus in every part of our lives.

One key to understanding how this works is to recognize that everything in liturgy is more than it seems. That is, everything in the liturgy is symbolic. Like John's gospel, or the words of a poem, or the objects in a painting, the liturgy represents both what it is and something deeper. Word is not just "word," but the word of God. Water is not just water, but the water of life. Light is not just light, but the light of Christ. Every word, gesture, song, action, and object is part of a living story. It is the story of our faith in Jesus.

✠ Symbol ✠

To understand how the liturgy trains our religious imagination, you have to understand how symbols work. Most of us already know instinctively how symbols work, but we don't think about it too much. So let's look at an example.

> Aleki Taumoepeau, an ecologist from New Zealand, was at work on a boat in Wellington harbor. Somehow, his wedding ring slipped off his finger and into the murky water. He tossed an anchor overboard to mark the spot and turned to Rachel, his bride of three months, with panic in his eyes. She told him not to worry about it; she'd buy him a new one. "No," he said. "I'll find it." He returned three months later with diving equipment and searched and searched. Yet, he was unable to find the ring. But he didn't give up. He went back again, a year later, and dove into the chilly, midwinter water. He was having no more success than the first time. He was cold and tired and near despair. He prayed, "God, it would be really good to find the ring about now." And then he spotted the anchor—with the ring lying right next to it. (http://www.boston.com/news/nation/articles/2009/08/20/persistence_helps_nz_diver_find_lost_wedding_ring/8/30/2009)

What do you think about Aleki? Is he crazy? Would you have done the same thing in his place? What made him do it? The cost of the ring was probably less than the cost of the two diving expeditions to recover it. Why not just purchase a duplicate ring?

We know the answer. The ring is not just any ring. It is a symbolic ring. That ring is unique among all other rings in the word. Its value isn't measured in dollars or appearance. The value comes from the promises that Aleki and Rachel made to each other as she first placed the ring on his finger. At that moment, the ring was still a ring, but it was also more. It became a part of their love for each other. At the same time, the ring points to the deep mystery of their love that can never be fully explained with mere words.

Now try to explain the idea of a wedding ring to someone who is completely unfamiliar with the custom and who heard Aleki's story. "It's a symbol of love and commitment," we might say.

"But isn't he still in love and still committed?" the inquirer might ask. "Why does he need the ring?"

"Well, he doesn't *need* the ring to be married," you might reply. "It's just very, very important."

"What makes it important? So important that he goes diving in cold murky water, twice, to find it?"

How would you answer? I'm not sure I know how I would answer. I don't know if I could come up with a complete, satisfactory answer to someone who didn't know anything about wedding rings.

It's like that, in a way, with the symbols of the liturgy. We don't always use expensive materials to celebrate the liturgy. But they have a lot of value. The things we do with them, the words we say, the actions we take, all have a literal, surface meaning. And liturgical symbols mean much more than just what is on the surface. The deeper meaning conveys the mystery of Jesus' love and our love for each other.

In the liturgy, the things we use all have deep symbolic meaning. Aleki's wedding ring is a symbol that conveys the love he and his wife have for each other. Their love, present in the ring, is the ring's true meaning. And the ring is unique. No other ring—even an exact duplicate—can convey that love in the same way. That's why he went to such lengths to find it. The ring actually became part of the love it symbolizes. Symbols in the liturgy function the same way. They are part of the reality they are signifying. When we use symbols that convey the love and mystery of Jesus, we "see" Jesus because he is present in the symbols and ritual of the liturgy.

The key to understanding how liturgy trains us to see Jesus everywhere is to understand that liturgy is symbolic and the symbols are filled with the reality of Jesus' love.

✠ How to read the symbols ✠

A symbol is, first of all, what it says it is. A ring might be a symbol of love and marriage, but it is first of all a ring. It never stops being a ring. In fact, without its "ringness," it couldn't be a symbol of love. If Aleki had dropped his ring into a metal crusher instead of the harbor, it would no longer be a symbol of his marriage because it would no longer be a ring.

Next, the quality of the symbol matters. We've all heard stories of people who have gotten married using cigar bands as their wedding ring, but have you ever actually seen one on someone's finger? The rings I see are gold or silver. Some have diamonds. They aren't all expensive, but none of them are cheap or flimsy. The quality of the ring matters to couples, and they spend a lot of time choosing rings that are exactly right. Care and even sacrifice need to go into the choosing of the symbol.

Then there is the presence level of the symbol. It is what makes the symbol unique. Aleki's ring had a quality about it that no other ring can ever have. It had the presence of his love of Rachel and his commitment to her. The ring doesn't "contain" his love, but it is a very real part of his love. The ring points to the great big, unexplainable, uncontainable love he has for Rachel. And while the ring is pointing to that mystery, it is also a part of the mystery.

There is one more important thing to understand about these symbols. The full meaning of a symbol is not in the thing itself. A symbol's full meaning is in what we do with it. So a ring is not just jewelry. A bridegroom *places* it, as a pledge, on his bride's finger as he makes a promise, and vice versa.

This is how we "read" symbols. We use them in particular ways, in a particular order, that is very much like a language. The symbols themselves and the things we do with the symbols speak to us the way the words of a story speak.

✢ Primary symbols ✢

In the liturgy, the story the symbols tell is a love story—the love of Jesus and the church. There are many symbols in the liturgy, but only a relative few that been handed down since the early beginnings of the church. Some long-time Catholics might argue that my list is missing one or two or that I've included one or two too many. There isn't a master list of symbols somewhere. But based on the way we celebrate liturgy, these are the primary symbols we use:

1. Water

2. Cross (crucifix, sign of the cross)

3. Light (candles, fire)

4. Oil

5. Word (book, spoken word, sung word, prayers, Scripture)

6. Altar

7. Bread

8. Wine (cup)

9. Assembly of people (bodies, gestures, congregation, priest, deacon, catechumens)

And remember, it is not just the symbols that are important, but their associated actions as well. Water is not just decoration. We *use it* to baptize and bless. The cross doesn't just hang on the wall. We process with it, sign ourselves with it, and mark other people and objects with it. All of our liturgical symbols are actions as much as objects.

✢ Water ✢

Let's look at the first symbol a little more. I grew up in St. Louis. Even before global warming, St. Louis was a very hot place to live in the summer. Because of that, I loved going to the community swimming pool. I wasn't a great swimmer. In fact, I don't think I swam much at all. Mostly, I would run to the end of the diving board and cannonball into the water, trying as best I could to aim my splash toward my younger brothers. If kids see a lot of water, it acts like a magnet. Children can't resist it.

The first year I worked in a parish, I was reminded of how much fun water is for kids. In that parish, we used a lot of water to baptize. We would immerse, or dunk, the babies completely underwater to baptize them. One of my jobs was to prepare everything for the Sunday afternoon baptisms we celebrated six times a year. We'd have about ten to fifteen families at each one, and they would bring relatives, neighbors, and older siblings and cousins of the infant. Some of the families would show up early, as I was still getting everything ready. I'd bring out a giant pottery bowl, place it on a stand, floor level, in front of the pews. The children would always come up to the bowl after I'd filled it with water. Some of the more active kids would put their hands in and swish the water around. A mom would usually rush forward, looking embarrassed, and hush the child back to his seat. And almost always, one of the grandmothers would make her way to the bowl when she thought I wasn't looking. She'd dip in a finger or press her wrist against the surface of the water.

These families were all engaging with the water at different levels. For the kids, the water was joy. It was something to play in, something that made them happy and filled them with life—like my childhood swimming pool.

For some of the moms, the water was a worry. It was a temptation to their children, and it could spill and make a mess.

For a long time, I couldn't figure out what Grandma was doing. And then I remembered something my own grandmother used to say to me when I wanted to go play in the rain. "Put on your boots and raincoat, or you'll catch your death of cold." Grandma—who probably thought dunking a naked baby in a vat of water right there in front of God and everybody was not a very Catholic thing to do—was checking the temperature. If her grandchild was going to get soaking wet, she wanted to be sure the baby wouldn't catch its "death of cold."

Water, especially if you have a lot of water, can mean different things to different people. It can mean happiness, life, worry, messiness, and even death. A good symbol doesn't have just one meaning. It has lots of meanings, some of which might even be contradictory. From early on, the church realized water was a powerful symbol for baptism because it could symbolize both dying to a former way of life and being born into a new life in Jesus. At the Easter Vigil each year, before the catechumens are baptized, we read something Saint Paul wrote to the ancient church in Rome:

> Are you unaware that we who were baptized into Christ Jesus were baptized into his death? We were indeed buried with him through baptism into death, so that, just as Christ was raised from the dead by the glory of the Father, we too might live in newness of life. (Romans 6:3–4)

So the water is like a tomb. The catechumen is buried in the water, ideally going completely under as I did doing my cannonballs. And then the catechumen is raised up out of the water, just as Jesus was raised out of the tomb, to new life. The tomb becomes a womb, giving a "second birth" to a new Christian.

Why don't we rebaptize other Christians who are becoming Catholic?

We never rebaptize anyone who has already been validly baptized in a Christian church. Baptism is like the example of Aleki and Rachel's wedding ring. There is only one ring, and there is only one baptism. If the baptism is "lost" or "forgotten," that doesn't make it any less real.

- Describe God as best you can.

- Do you have something unique, like a wedding ring, that can never be replaced? What does it symbolize for you?

- Choose a symbol, other than water, from the list above, and write as many meanings of it as you can think of.

See the world with Catholic eyes

CATHOLICS DON'T RESTRICT THE USE OF SYMBOLS only to the liturgy. We also use symbols as lenses through which to see the world. There is a story in the Bible that is a good example of what I mean.

> Some people brought a blind man to [Jesus] and begged him to touch him. He took the blind man by the hand and led him out of the village; and when he had put saliva on his eyes and laid his hands on him, he asked him, "Can you see anything?" And the man looked up and said, "I can see people, but they look like trees, walking." Then Jesus laid his hands on his eyes again; and he looked intently and his sight was restored, and he saw everything clearly. (Mark 8:22–26)

That story always fascinates me. Why did Jesus have to lay his hands on the blind man's eyes twice? You'd think the Son of God could get it right the first time, wouldn't you? Remember, though, many of the stories in the Bible are symbolic—they have several layers of meaning. This is a story about Jesus, but it is also a story about the followers of Jesus. We don't always "see" everything all at once. It takes some time to learn to see clearly. Faith is a miracle, but growing in faith is a discipline.

As we grow in faith and practice the disciplines of the faith, we start to see the world differently. There are four primary disciplines of Christian life that shape how we see. They are the disciplines of worship, word, community life, and service to the poor. We're going to spend some extra time looking at worship because Catholics believe what we do in the liturgy shapes the way we act in the world. We'll look at the other three disciplines a little later.

✠ Worship ✠

The more we praise God in the liturgy and see more and more deeply into the symbols of the liturgy, the more we begin to see the meaning of those symbols in everyday life. For example, the way we use water and tell stories about water from the Bible in the liturgy trains us to see water differently. We see God's love for us in the waters of baptism, and then we begin to see God's love for us in the water that is all around us. A dripping faucet, a warm morning shower, a backyard creek, a puddle from a spring rain are filled with God's love. We see God in the power of the ocean, the pounding of a thunderstorm, and the cascade of a waterfall. We remember our baptism in the water. We remember the Scripture stories of creation, the great flood, the parting of the sea, and Jesus walking on water. We begin to see more clearly that much of the world is thirsty, that clean water is not a basic and available resource in many places, that people's lives and homes have been flooded away.

According to UNICEF, 884 million people in the world do not have access to safe water. This is roughly one in eight of the world's population. The United Nations Development Programme reports that 1.8 million children die every year as a result of diseases caused by unclean water and poor sanitation. This amounts to around 5,000 deaths a day. Organizations such as Catholic Relief Services and Living Water International work with people of faith to respond to this desperate need. (Source: http://www.water.cc/living-water/resources/)

That's the idea, anyway. I'd like to say I think all those deep thoughts every time a busboy sloshes an icy glass onto my table or I wash some vegetables before cooking. I don't. Most times, I don't even think about water because it is so common. But once in a while, I notice. Once in a while, I realize what water really means, on all the deep levels of symbol and mystery. And slowly, drip by drip, what I have learned about water in the liturgy begins to shape me. On any given day, I don't notice any difference. But I see a difference in my life now and my life five years ago. I see a huge difference from twenty and thirty years ago.

Water is just one of the key symbols. Each of the others works in a similar way, on many levels at once, to shape our lives, slowly, day by day, teaching us to be more and more like Jesus.

✠ The story ✠

The liturgy doesn't just throw symbols at us, hoping some of them stick. The liturgy is a giant story, with smaller stories wrapped up within it. To help us see how this works, we'll look at one part of our liturgy—the Sunday Mass—and show how it is similar to Thanksgiving dinner.

We think of Thanksgiving dinner as the meal itself. But really, there is more to it than just eating. We can think of Thanksgiving as having four parts. Everyone gathers at Grandma's house; as we gather, we chat with each other, tell stories, and catch up on family news; then we eat; and finally, we all return home, reunited as a family.

Similarly, the Sunday Mass has four parts:

1. Introduction: God gathers the people

2. Part I: God speaks to the people

3. Part II: The people thank God

4. Conclusion: The people go out to do God's work

(See the appendix for a full outline.)

✠ Introduction ✠

The introduction, the gathering, is very important. Ask yourself why we would have to come together for God to speak to us. Can't God speak to us individually? Recall the Thanksgiving dinner we started with. Couldn't we all catch up on family news or share stories by e-mail or on Facebook? What is the difference when we are together as a family and when we are alone? Usually, a family feels stronger and more complete when everyone is together. And we are more recognizable as a family to others as well.

When we gather as God's family, we become one of the primary symbols we talked about earlier. We become an assembly of people, gathered for a purpose. We become the body of Christ, each of us having a role and a place in the body—just as an eye and a hand and a foot all have a job in a body. At Thanksgiving, do you notice if someone is missing? The family feels incomplete, and we hope maybe next year everyone can make it. In a similar way, we all have to be at Sunday Mass or else the body is incomplete.

The introduction or the introductory rites is everything from the opening song until the opening prayer, which is said just before we sit down to hear the readings. Next time you are at Mass, pay attention to everything that happens in this part of the Mass. Ask yourself, what are we doing that makes us one? What are we doing that gathers us? What are we doing that makes us ready for God to speak to us?

✠ Part I: God speaks to the people ✠

The reason we come together is so God can speak to us. "Speech," or "word," is one of the primary symbols. We hear God's word in lots of ways. The clearest, most complete way is when parts of the Bible are read at Sunday Mass. Christians believe God's word is a "living word." That means that even though we are listening to something that was written thousands of years ago, there is a living spirit in those words that is supposed to shape us. This is very similar to the stories we tell in our family gatherings. My mother tells me stories about my father, who died when I was very young. She tells me stories about her parents and what it was like when she was a little girl. I've heard some of these stories many times, but they always seem new to me. I can feel the presence of those family members who are no longer with us.

Of course, I'm speaking about ideal situations again. I'd like to think that I have a deeply spiritual experience every time I hear the readings at Mass. Sometimes, though, I'm worried about my next deadline or trying to remember what I have to pick up from the store. Or sometimes the reader is so bad or so boring I can't really pay attention. There's nothing magic about the readings. Just because they are biblical doesn't mean mountains quake and oceans swell each time we open the book. We have to pay attention and contemplate what it is God might be saying to us. We have to listen.

Here is an important point about how Catholics listen to God's word, however. It doesn't all depend upon me. In the liturgy, God is speaking to us as a community. If I'm not paying attention or if I'm confused, I can rely on the rest of the assembly to "hear" with me. What is most important is how we all listen together, as a community.

Of course, as a participating member of the community, it is still important that I focus as best I can as an individual. And even though I'm often inattentive and distracted, I do *hear*. Over time, God's word fills my heart, and I am changed. Just as the symbol of water shapes us, drip by drip, day by day, we hear God's word, deep in our hearts, and it changes us.

Conversion

You will probably hear a lot about **conversion** *during your preparation process. In one way, conversion is easy to understand. Conversion means change. When you "change money," you are converting dollars* *to pesos, for example. When a caterpillar changes into a butterfly, it is converting from one form of life to another.*

For the unbaptized person, you will have a very significant conversion, like the caterpillar. You will change from being outside of the body of Christ and into being a member of the body of Christ.

For the baptized, non-practicing person, you will also experience a significant conversion, but your conversion won't be the caterpillar-to-butterfly kind. You are already a "butterfly." You are already a Christian. You may not have felt like or acted like a Christian ever before in your life, but now you are beginning that journey. But the "change" has already happened in you. Now you will begin to realize what it is to live as who you truly are.

Baptized, practicing Christians also talk about an "ongoing conversion." What we mean by that is that in one way, conversion is a one-time event. Before we were not part of the body. Then, at our baptism, we were once and forever changed. But in another way, we are always going deeper into that change. While conversion is a one-time event, it is also an ongoing process of growing in faith and becoming a better and better Christian over the course of our lives.

✛ Part II: The people thank God ✛

God's love is pure gift. We can't do enough good things to earn it. And one of the really infuriating things to those of us who like to keep score is, we can't really do enough bad things to unearn it. We usually refer to God as "Father," but for my money, God is much more like my mother. When we were growing up, I was the good child. I'm the oldest, and my mother impressed on me my responsibility to set an example. I wasn't perfect, but I tried to live up to Mom's expectations. (I still try to!) My youngest brother, on the other hand, is a different story. Especially when he was a teenager, he seemed determined to break every rule and challenge every boundary. So who do you think my mom loves? *Both of us!*

Does my brother deserve my mother's love? Probably not. But then, neither do I, when you think about it. Mom doesn't love me for the things I do right. She loves me because I'm me. And she loves my brother because he's who he is. Neither of us ever have to do a thing to "earn" her love.

In Part I of the liturgy, when God speaks to us, we're mostly hearing stories about how much God loves us. As we hear those stories and as we are changed by them, we're overcome with a powerful sense of gratitude. Maybe I'm not *personally* being overcome on a given Sunday, but as a whole, over time, the church is flooded with joy and gratitude for the gift of God's love. The proper response to a gift is to say, "Thank you."

And that's exactly what we do in Part II. The ritual name for this second part of the liturgy is "Eucharist," which is Greek for "thanksgiving."

The meal part of the Mass is the part that most clearly resembles Thanksgiving dinner. Our American ancestors gave thanks for their life in a new land by sharing a meal. And Jesus told us to give thanks also by sharing a meal. The way in which we participate most fully in the thanksgiving of the Eucharist is by sharing in Communion. Catholics believe that in the celebration of the Mass, the bread and wine are changed into the Body and Blood of Christ. (Recall how Aleki's ring was changed from an ordinary ring into a real part of his love for Rachel.) And when we eat and drink the Body and Blood of Christ, we are also changed. St. Augustine said we become what we eat. This action in the liturgy is a direct response to Jesus' command to break bread and share the cup as a sign of sharing in his body and blood. Several things happen to us when we share in Communion:

1. Our union with Christ is strengthened
2. Our spirit is nourished
3. We are separated from sin
4. We become more loving
5. We become one with each other, as church
6. We become more committed to the poor

When I was a child, I was taught that when I shared in Communion, Christ was "in" me. I used to think that meant that before Communion, he was somehow not in me. A more nuanced understanding is to say that through sharing in the Body and Blood of Christ, the Spirit of Christ grows stronger in us and Christ becomes more present in us in the ways listed above. These six ways in which Jesus becomes stronger and more present in us, especially the strengthening of our commitment to the poor, lead us to the final part of the liturgy.

Conclusion:
✴ The people go out to do God's work ✴

The conclusion to the Mass is meant to be very abrupt. It consists of a final blessing and a formal dismissal of the assembly. Sometimes we add announcements and singing at the end, but, strictly speaking, those are not part of the conclusion. The way the ritual is given to us in the official rite is that after the dismissal, we simply leave. Why so abrupt?

In the Mass, if we have been actively listening to God's word for us in the liturgy, and if we have been truly thankful for God's total love for us, we can't help but be changed. So when we leave the liturgy, we are going back out into the world more united as Christians—people more like Jesus. If we are more like Jesus, that means we will want to continue the work Jesus started. And the work of Jesus is so urgent that the Mass ends quickly—so we can start the work of Jesus more quickly. That is, we will want to rush out to tell more and more people about the overwhelming love of God. That doesn't necessarily mean you stop people on street corners and quote Scripture to them. There are lots of ways to tell people about God's love. Communicating God's love is a lifestyle, a way of living. It is the Jesus way. If you want to become a Catholic, your preparation process will be all about learning to live that way.

Of course, the liturgy assumes we are ideal Christians, always seeking to become more and more like Christ. And, when we look at the entire church throughout history, that's true. But any single person, on any single day, struggles to live up to the ideal. Often we fail. Even so, living the disciplines of the Christian lifestyle helps us get closer and closer to who Christ calls us to be.

As we mentioned earlier, there are four disciplines involved in living the Jesus way: worship, word, community, and service to the poor. We already looked at worship a little bit. In the next chapters, we will say more about worship and also examine word, community, and service.

Catechumens

If you are a catechumen, you are dismissed before we get to Part II of the Mass. Your dismissal has both a symbolic meaning and a practical purpose. The symbolic meaning is linked to one of the primary symbols listed earlier—the gathered assembly.

Any assembly has an order to it. A Thanksgiving dinner is a family assembly, and everyone has a role. Someone cooks the turkey. Someone brings the wine. Someone is the carver. There is a children's table and an adults' table. Often, when there are family disagreements at Thanksgiving, it is because someone in the family is acting "out of order."

Something similar happens when we gather for Sunday liturgy. In the liturgy, just as at a family dinner, everyone has a role to play. There are four major roles in the Mass and then smaller roles within those roles. The four major roles, or orders, are:

    1. Order of the presbyterate (priests)
    2. Order of the diaconate
    3. Order of the faithful
    4. Order of the catechumenate

The role of the order of the catechumenate is to hear God's word. The role of the other three orders is to also hear God's word and then to work together to offer ritual thanksgiving for the gift of God's love. Since ritual thanksgiving is not part of the role of the catechumens, they are dismissed after they have done their job. Once the catechumens are baptized, they will take on new roles and responsibilities. The symbolic meaning is that we are not just a random gathering of people. We are an assembly with a job to do.

There is also a practical function. The catechumens are not just dismissed to go to the mall or watch the game. They go to another nearby place and continue doing their listening job. After the homily, usually with the help of one of the members of the order of the faithful, the catechumens reflect on the readings they just heard. They try to hear the deeper meaning in God's word. They try to discern how, through these readings, God is speaking directly to them. That is the primary function of the order of the catechumenate.

Baptized candidates

If you are already baptized and you want to become Catholic or complete your initiation as a Catholic, you might be in a formation group that includes catechumens. Even though you are hanging out with them, you are in two different orders. Because of your baptism, even though it might not have been in a Catholic church, you are already a member of the order of the faithful. Maybe you already knew that or sensed that. Perhaps that's one of the factors in your decision to become a Catholic or complete your initiation.

Or maybe your baptism never really meant that much to you. Maybe you feel much more like a member of the order of the catechumenate than a member of the order of the faithful.

It's okay to feel that way. But at the same time, you need to start thinking about what it means to you to be in the order of the faithful. You can't ever go back to not being one of the faithful. So if you're baptized, whether you want to be or not, you have to start doing the work of the order of the faithful. Your role is to pray for others, which we do in the intercessions or "prayer of the faithful." Also, the faithful give ritual thanks to God, which we do in the eucharistic prayer.

However, because you are not yet Catholic, you are not yet in full communion with the rest of the Catholics. Or, if you are Catholic, but haven't celebrated your first Communion, you cannot yet share at the altar. That means you can do almost everything the fully initiated Catholics do, except actually share in Communion. There is a lot that happens in Part II besides Communion, but Communion is the climax. As a baptized person, you can participate in all the thanksgiving prayers and actions that take place right up to the moment of Communion.

So, in some parishes, because the baptized candidates cannot yet fully participate in Communion, they are dismissed along with the catechumens. In other parishes, the pastor or the leader of the initiation process leaves it up to the baptized candidate to decide if he or she wants to stay or be dismissed.

And in my parish, because we believe so strongly in the role and work of the order of the faithful, the baptized candidates would always remain in the assembly for the entire liturgy. When the catechumens are dismissed and the baptized candidates remain, their continued presence in the assembly is a strong symbol that teaches us the meaning of baptism. Because of their baptism, the candidates not only have a right to remain in the assembly, they have a responsibility to share in the work of the baptized.

- What has been your experience of the first part of the Mass (introduction and liturgy of the word)? What have you noticed? What intrigues you? What questions do you have?

- If you have not yet been present for the second part of the Mass, what are you looking forward to? What do you wonder about? If you have been present, what have you noticed? What has been most memorable?

- If you are unbaptized, how would you describe God's role in your life? If you are baptized, describe how you see yourself as already part of the order of the faithful, a full member of the Body of Christ.

Live a life of worship

MY MOM WAS A SINGLE MOM from the time I was four, and there were three of us boys. She made sure we were at Mass every Sunday. And I have to tell you, my brothers did not make it easy for her. (I, of course, was a model child!) Seriously, between lost shoes, cranky children, and a not-too-reliable Volkswagen, it's a wonder we were ever at Mass. I didn't much want to go to Mass when I was a kid. But now, looking back, I can see that my family's regular participation in the liturgy is probably the most significant part of my faith formation. It is difficult to overstate this. You can miss a few catechetical sessions. You can miss a few parish activities. But you cannot miss Sunday Mass. When I was a kid, I was taught that this is a rule. But it is more than just a rule. It is the key way in which we celebrate and deepen our faith.

The reason it is so important for you to be in church on Sunday is that your hearing of the word prepares you for what your next job will be. If you are unbaptized, after your baptism, you will be part of the order of the faithful.

And if you are already baptized, you have a job as a member of the order of the faithful. That job is to join with the community to offer praise and thanksgiving to God. If you're not there, just as if a family member is missing at Thanksgiving dinner, the assembly is incomplete.

Home study vs. conversion

I know you're going to ask, so let's get it out on the table right now. If you have to miss a Sunday, can't you just read the readings for that day? Won't that form you in God's word? Well, it's better than nothing, but it's a far distant second best. Here's why. Your job is not to **read** *God's word. It is to* **hear** *God's word in the midst of the assembly.*

When my mom was trying to herd us kids together, sometimes she'd lose her patience. If I was the one delaying us, she'd say pretty loudly, "Nicholas, you never listen to me!" Now she and I both knew I'd physically heard every word she said. But I hadn't taken her words to heart. Her words had not converted me from inaction to action. In that sense, I was deaf to what she was asking me to do.

God's word works in a similar way. Hearing is not simply about knowing what words are in the Bible. Hearing is paying attention to God in such a profound way that it changes us. We're moved to do something because we really heard God's call deep in our hearts. And that call comes to us first of all as members of the body of Christ—an assembly of people. God's call comes most clearly and consistently to us when we are gathered in worship.

It took me a lot of years to learn that, but I finally did. We'd get to Mass every Sunday, often a few minutes late, and tumble into the pew. Mom would be shushing us as she peeled off our coats and separated us from each other so we wouldn't poke and distract each other. And once we were all settled in, she made it very, very clear we were to **pay attention**. *I was well into adulthood before I realized my job was to do more than just pay attention. And after my first year in parish ministry, I realized we all have a lot of work to do.*

Before I worked in a parish, I didn't realize the amount of work that goes into preparing Sunday liturgy. And I discovered most people come to Mass expecting to get something out of it—like when they go to a movie or a play expecting to be entertained.

Much of your formation will be focused on a different attitude. Instead of learning what to get from the Mass, you will be learning how to **prepare** *for the liturgy, learning how to* **participate** *in the liturgy, and learning how to* **act** *on your experience of the liturgy. This is especially true for the unbaptized and the non-practicing baptized folks.*

If you are baptized and have been a pretty active Christian, you may know how to do this already. Your job is to model for others how to prepare for and participate in the liturgy.

✳ Preparation ✳

Sunday liturgy doesn't happen just on Sunday. For Catholics, our whole week is about Sunday. We are either reflecting on and acting on what we experienced, or we are preparing for the next Sunday liturgy. Preparation involves becoming better and better at hearing God's call. You are going to do that through prayer and reading God's word at home and throughout the week.

Prayer

An excellent resource for someone just beginning to pray is *The Catholic Way to Pray: An Essential Guide for Adults* by Kathleen Glavich, SND (Twenty-Third Publications). She deals with some misperceptions about prayer and also gives suggestions for the best times for prayer. There are at least three important times you should pray every day: in the morning, before meals, and before going to bed.

Scripture

I know I said reading Scripture is not the same as hearing God's word, but I didn't say reading Scripture was unimportant. In fact, you need to read Scripture on a regular basis to help you hear God's word better. You should have a Bible and the list of readings for the upcoming Sunday. On at least one day during the week, prayerfully read over the readings for the coming Sunday. You can also read the readings online, but it is better if you read them from the Bible. That way, you'll learn where all the different books of the Bible are, and you'll learn how to navigate through it. To find a list of the readings for the coming Sunday, check in your parish bulletin or go to usccb.org/nab.

I already have a Bible. Can I use that?

Much of the Old Testament was written in ancient Hebrew, and the New Testament was written in first-century Greek. Obviously, for us to be able to read it, someone needed to translate it into English (or whatever language we read). If you speak more than one language, you know that not all translations convey even simple messages the same way. If I'm translating the word "car" from English to Spanish, for example, I can use **carro** *or* **coche**. *Which is the better translation? That depends on where you are from—Mexico or Spain.*

However, since you want to grow in your Catholic identity, you will want to begin to use a translation that is at home in our tradition.

If you are from an evangelical tradition, you are probably used to the **King James Version**. *Many contemporary evangelicals use the* **New International Version** *(NIV). A Catholic translation that might be a good fit for you is the* **New Jerusalem Bible**.

If you come from a mainline Protestant tradition, you are probably most familiar with the **New Revised Standard Version** *(NRSV). The NRSV is also approved by the Catholic Church for study and prayer.*

In Catholic worship in the United States, we use the **New American Bible** *(NAB). So if you want to read from a Bible that uses the same words you hear at Mass, get a* **New American Bible**.

If you make a regular practice of daily prayer and read the readings for Sunday before you come to church, you'll be much better prepared for the liturgy. You'll be able to do more than just pay attention. You'll be able to fully engage with the assembly and with the Lord when you hear God's call.

✤ Participation ✤

I'm going to focus on our participation in the liturgy of the word. If you are baptized and not dismissed after the word, ask your sponsor and initiation team for guidance on participating in the second part of the liturgy.

You can learn everything you need to know about participating in the liturgy of word by imitating your sponsor. I'll just touch on a few things briefly here.

Posture

The liturgy of the word begins with a change in posture. From the moment the Mass begins, we are standing. The opening rites conclude with the opening prayer. At the end of the prayer, we sit, and the liturgy of the word begins with the first reading. We remain seated for the first reading, the psalm (which is sung), and the second reading. Then we stand for the gospel acclamation and the gospel. Standing signifies that the gospel is the most important reading in the liturgy of the word. It is most important because we will be hearing the story of Jesus from the gospels. And we believe that when we hear the gospels proclaimed in the liturgy, we are hearing Jesus speak to us. After the proclamation of the gospel, we sit for the homily.

Eye contact

A clear way to show your participation in the liturgy of the word is to maintain eye contact with whoever is speaking or leading the singing. You may notice a lot of the Catholics around you reading along in booklets. If I could sit my mother down next to them, she'd lean over and whisper, "Put that away, and pay attention." Paying attention is not reading along with the reader. Paying attention is engaging the reader in a nonverbal dialogue, always listening for the Spirit speaking deep in our hearts as we do so. If you've prepared well by reading the readings ahead of time, you won't need to follow along, with your head buried in a worship booklet.

In some cultures, making direct eye contact might be seen as a sign of disrespect. If that's true for you, participate nonverbally in the way that is most comfortable. For most of us, though, the general rule is that we make eye contact and pay attention.

Singing

I've heard so many Catholics say, "I don't sing," that I've lost count. That's like a baseball player saying, "I don't throw." Singing is a requirement of liturgy, and it is one of the most important ways we pray. So a key marker of your participation in the liturgy of the word will be singing. Singing is a sign of unity with those around us. Singing also lifts the spirit and expresses emotion in a unique way.

There are at least two times to sing in the Liturgy of the Word: the response to the psalm and the acclamation for the gospel.

Gesture

The most common gesture you will make during the liturgy of the word is a triple sign of the cross. It comes just before the gospel when the reader says: "A reading from the holy gospel according to Mark" (or Matthew, Luke, or John). We respond, "Glory to you, O Lord." At the same time, using the right thumb, we make a sign of the cross on our forehead, lips, and heart. This is a physical way of asking God to open our minds, lips, and heart to the message of the gospel.

Action

Our preparation for and participation in the liturgy of the word is all for one purpose—to move us to action. For those in the order of the faithful, that action is twofold. First, we gather at the table of the Lord to break bread and share the cup. We do this because Jesus told us to. But our action doesn't stop there. Jesus wanted us to remember him by breaking bread and sharing the cup so that we would go out from Mass to offer Jesus to the world. One of the things you will learn as a catechumen is what that action in the world looks like. We'll say more about that in a later chapter.

- Why is participating in Sunday liturgy important to you?

- What do you currently do to prepare for participating in the Sunday liturgy? What else could you do?

- How does your participation in the Sunday liturgy change the way you live during the rest of the week?

Live the word

THE NEXT AREA OF CHRISTIAN LIFE we need to look at is living the word of God. Let's explore more deeply what we mean by the word of God.

✠ Metaphor ✠

First of all, like the liturgy, the word of God is symbolic. The very idea of God speaking to us is a metaphor. When we say God spoke to us, we don't usually mean we heard an actual voice that could be tape recorded. Here's an example of how someone thousands of years ago heard God "speak" in a thunderstorm:

Bless the Lord, my soul!
Lord God, how great you are,
clothed in majesty and glory,
wrapped in light as in a robe!

You stretch out the heavens like a tent.
Above the rains you build your dwelling.
You make the clouds your chariot,
you walk on the wings of the wind,
you make the winds your messengers
and flashing fire your servants.

You founded the earth on its base,
to stand firm from age to age.
You wrapped it with the ocean like a cloak:
the waters stood higher than the mountains.

At your threat they took to flight;
at the voice of your thunder they fled.
They rose over the mountains and flowed down
to the place which you had appointed.
You set limits they might not pass
lest they return to cover the earth.

You make springs gush forth in the valleys;
they flow in between the hills.
They give drink to all the beasts of the field;
the wild asses quench their thirst.
On their banks dwell the birds of heaven;
from the branches they sing their song.

From your dwelling you water the hills;
earth drinks its fill of your gift.
You make the grass grow for the cattle
and the plants to serve our needs,

that he may bring forth bread from the earth
and wine to cheer our heart;
oil, to make our face shine
and bread to strengthen our heart.
(Psalm 104, The Grail Psalter, 1993 revision)

Obviously, God doesn't wear a robe or live in a tent. He doesn't ride around on cloud chariots or use lightning as Fed Ex agents. Thunder isn't literally the voice of God. And yet, if we believe God is everywhere, and we have been trained to see the world symbolically, we can, indeed, "see" and "hear" God in a thunderstorm.

A thunderstorm is, in fact, a relatively easy place in which to see God. A tremendous sound and light show that seems more powerful than anything human can be quite a religious experience. It is more difficult to see God in the day-to-day grind of our ordinary lives. And still more difficult to find God's presence in places where people are ill or oppressed or mistreated.

God in the silence

There is a story in the Old Testament about the prophet Elijah. He felt abandoned by God and could not find God in tornado-like winds, a powerful earthquake, or a raging fire. Finally, he found God in "a sound of sheer silence" (1 Kings 19:12).

And that brings us to the primary role of those who are in the order of the catechumenate. The primary job of the catechumens is to hear God's word—even when it is difficult to hear. So if your primary job is to hear God's word, and God isn't physically speaking, what are you supposed to listen for? Or, to ask the question another way, how does God speak?

And before that question, we might want to ask, *why* does God speak? The answer to that question is easy to give, but not always easy to accept. God is always speaking to us because God is crazy in love with us. And God wants us to be in love back. Were you ever smitten with someone who didn't know you existed? I knew a kid in high school who was completely besotted with a cute redhead. And she'd paid him no attention. So what did the boy do? Everything he could think of to get the girl to notice him. And that's how God is. God is constantly trying to get our attention.

> ### God is love
>
> *My dear friends, let us love one another, since love is from God and everyone who loves is a child of God and knows God. Whoever fails to love does not know God, because God is love. This is the revelation of God's love for us, that God sent his only Son into the world that we might have life through him. (1 John 4:7–9,* **New Jerusalem Bible***)*

That seems counterintuitive to many of us. Many of us think of God as distant and absent. Aren't we the ones that are always looking for God and coming up empty? Not really. That redheaded girl would get together with her girlfriends and complain that there were no cute, fun boys in our school. She just wasn't paying attention. We are usually the redheaded girl, not paying attention to all the ways in which God is trying to get our attention.

That's why your number-one job as a catechumen is to hear God's word. The catechumenate is a training process to help you pay attention. These are some of the ways God speaks to us that you will have to pay attention to.

✠ Bible ✠

Many people think that everything God ever said is in the Bible. And they think God said everything all at once, all in order, like a rec⸱ book for living a holy life. It's not quite like that. The Bible is r⸱ a bookshelf of Really Important Books that lots of peor⸱ decided we should pay attention to. From what we⸱ far, it will not be a surprise to learn that Cath⸱ God literally said every word that is in t⸱ believe that, but most do not. So how ⸱ didn't literally "say" what's in there?

Instead of thinking of the Bible as a transcript or a news report, think of it instead as a story. A lot of the Bible actually is written in story format, but some of it is not. Even so, the entire collection of books on the Really Important Books list is a kind of story. It is the story of God's actions, throughout history, to get our attention. At important moments throughout history, God's people actually did pay attention. Sometimes God had to do some amazing and dramatic stuff to get our attention, and those amazing things became stories that we told each other from generation to generation. Eventually the stories, laws, poems, songs, and histories got written down. The best of these, the most important, were collected together into what we call the Bible.

✛ Lectionary ✛

A lectionary is a book of "lections" or readings taken from the Bible. The Jewish people have an ancient tradition of reading passages from the books of Moses and the prophets in the synagogue on the Sabbath. Jesus grew up with this tradition, as did all of the first disciples. That tradition carried over into Christian worship from the very earliest times.

However, early Christians did not read only from the Jewish Scriptures. They also read from letters sent to their parishes by one of the leaders of the church (for example St. Paul or St. Peter) and from one of the gospels.

The lectionary began as simply a reference list of readings assigned to each Sunday that the reader would use to find the right place in the Bible to read from. Over time, it evolved into a book of actual readings, all taken from the Bible. Today, the lectionary is a multi-volume work that contains readings for all the Sundays, feasts, weekdays, and special celebrations of the church.

Most Catholics have never read the Bible cover to cover. The way Catholics "read" the Bible is by hearing it read at Sunday Mass.

Now I personally think Catholics should do a little more reading of the Bible on their own, but even if we did, Sunday Mass would still be the *primary* way we read or hear the Bible.

The lectionary draws from the Bible to make something crystal clear—everything God said in the Bible had one point. "Jesus" is everything God wants to say to us. So the lectionary is set up to tell us the complete story of how all of history was building up to the event of Jesus being born, living among us, dying, and rising. Every Sunday, we hear another small piece of that story by listening to selections of readings taken from the Bible. As catechumens, you're going to pay a lot of attention to the Bible, specifically as it is read at Sunday Mass. It would be good for you to read more of the Bible on your own as well, but keep in mind that the Sunday readings are the primary thing to pay attention to.

If you are baptized, non-practicing, you will also want to pay close attention to the word. Even though you are a member of the order of the faithful, you are just now beginning to understand how God's word leads us to the work of offering praise and thanksgiving.

And if you are baptized and have been active in your faith tradition, you likely already have a deep love for God's word. Depending on which tradition you come from, you may have to spend some time getting used to the liturgy as the *primary* place in which we encounter God's word.

✠ Church teaching ✠

If we believe that "Jesus" is what God wants to say to us, then where do we "hear" Jesus speaking? In the Bible for sure. And we also hear Jesus speaking through the church—the body of believers who continue to follow Jesus. If you've seen the movie *Fiddler on the Roof*, you have a sense of how this works. In the movie, Tevye the milkman sings about the value of tradition. And the rest of the story is about how the forces of history in 1905 bring rapid and unsettling changes to his small Jewish village. It seems he must abandon his traditions—God's Tradition! Knowing how to apply the traditions of our ancestors in the face of new circumstances is always difficult. It continues to be a challenge for God's people today. Catholics believe that the teaching authority of the church is guided by the Holy Spirit to help us know how to interpret, apply, and communicate ancient traditions in the twenty-first century. And so, as catechumens, you need to pay attention to what the church is teaching.

✠ Yourself ✠

God is also speaking through you. The Spirit of God is moving in you, and that is why you are here in the first place. So you must pay attention to what God is doing in you. As best you can, you have to be true to what God is calling you to and follow that call. This is very important because you then become the word of God for the rest of us. We see how God loves you and that tells us God loves us all. We "hear" God in you.

- How does God speak to you? How have you experienced God's word?

- What parts of the Bible have you read? What are a couple of your favorite Bible stories and why are they important to you?

- How do you think God speaks to people today?

Live in community

WHEN YOU WERE FIRST EXPLORING THE IDEA of becoming Catholic, what did you imagine "being Catholic" would be like? Sometimes "being Catholic" gets confused with "being religious." Even some of us who have been Catholic all our lives can get a little confused about this. Most people think of "being religious" as following a set of rules that will make them good people. And if they are good enough, they will go to heaven when they die. When I was growing up, that's pretty much what I thought "being Catholic" was about.

You probably realize by now that "being Catholic" is a lot deeper than that. A better way to understand "being Catholic" is to say that we are "being church." I like the word "church" because it is symbolic in the sense we talked about earlier.

The word "church" comes from Latin (*ecclesia*), which came from Greek (*ekkalein*). Its literal meaning is to "call out of." We said in the section on word that God speaks to us. It's more correct to say God *calls us* (out of darkness, out of our old way of living, out of hopelessness).

There are two ways to understand a call. The first is that someone is calling me personally, like a phone call. The second is that I'm being called to be part of something, like a call to service or a call to action. The call of God is both personal and bigger than personal. When we are talking about "being Catholic," though, the emphasis is on the bigger sense. This is a pretty important idea to understand as you go through the catechumenate. As I said, I didn't always understand it, and I grew up Catholic. I thought God was calling me, personally, to be good so I would go to heaven. But there is so much more to the call than that. God calls us as a community or as a body— all together.

That's where the "symbol" of church can help because it means God is calling all of us, all together. In the Bible, there are lots and lots of images for "church." If you look intently at the images when you encounter them, one after the other, they will begin to form you in a deeper understanding of what "being Catholic" looks like.

✠ Sheepfold ✠

Many places in the Bible talk about the sheep and a shepherd. God or Jesus is the shepherd, and we are the flock. One of the titles for Jesus is "Good Shepherd," who gave his life for the flock. And we are called to imitate the sacrifice of the shepherd.

✠ Field ✠

Other stories speak of the church as a field that grows olive trees or wheat or vineyards. Jesus is the true vine, and we are all branches of that vine. If we are cut off from Christ, like a pruned branch, we will die. Through the gift of baptism, we are grafted onto Christ, and then we can never die.

✠ Building ✠

We often think of the building we worship in as the church. Jesus used this image too. He said he was the cornerstone of the foundation. The church is built on that foundation. Another name for the building that is the church is "temple." God dwells in the temple that is not made of stone. That is, God dwells in us. And so, ultimately, the church is not just a building. The church is the also the people who gather in the building.

✠ Bride ✠

The church is often called the Bride of Christ, a spouse who is united with the Bridegroom forever.

There are several things that are common to each of these images. If we can draw out the commonalities, you'll have a pretty good idea of what it means to "be Catholic."

1. In each of these images, the church is united to and dependent upon Christ.
2. All of these images are about life. In fact, the opposites of these images are images of isolation or death.
3. All of these images are images of community. We cannot do the work of the church alone, and so the call is not solely a personal call. The call to life, the call out of death, is a call to join with the community of love.

✠ Body ✠

That brings us to the final image I want to point out. St. Paul says that we are a body. Christ is the head, and each of us are parts of the body. Like a human body, we all have a role to play. We can't say our role is unimportant because the body would not function as it should without each of its parts. Our call is a call out of loneliness and isolation and into the Body of Christ. Our job is not to be good so we will go to heaven. Our job is to work together to find the parts of the body that are missing and reconnect them or reconcile them with Christ.

Exactly *how* you do that is what you are supposed to be learning in the catechumenate. Ideally, your sponsor, your catechists, your pastor, and all the other members of the body—of the church—are doing this kind of work all the time. Your job during your formation is to watch them and imitate them. Here are some of the things to watch:

1. The way they pray—both at Mass and outside of Mass

2. How they talk about their faith—especially with those who are not yet part of the body

3. The way they keep their hopes up, even in difficult times, because they trust in Jesus

4. The way they listen to the Holy Spirit and follow where the Spirit leads them

5. The way they love other people—even people who are difficult to love

I'm not saying that every Catholic you meet is going to be great at all these things all the time. On a good day, I'm "great" at maybe one of them. And I'm not always having a good day. That's the point of being in a community. When I'm having a bad day, someone else in the community is stronger and doing better. That person helps me get better. Don't look at what any one individual is doing. Look at what the *body* is doing. That's what "being Catholic" is all about—what we do together.

- Have you ever been part of a team or a community? How is that similar and different from being part of a church?

- There are several images of church listed above. Which speaks to you most strongly? Can you think of any other images?

- What is it about being part of the Catholic community that is most important to you?

Serve the poor

HERE'S ANOTHER CATHOLIC WORD FOR YOU: *apostolic*. When you are baptized (or when you are received into full communion), you will profess your faith in the church that is "one, holy, catholic, and apostolic." You've probably heard of the apostles. "Apostle" is a Greek word that means "one who is sent." When we say the church is apostolic, we're saying we are a group of messengers.

So what's the message? It's the message you heard in the liturgy of the word. Of course, we hear the message (God's call) in lots of other ways as well. The liturgy of the word is the clearest and most profound way, however. And, as we said, the liturgy of the word is a call to do something. It is a call to go out into the world with the message we just heard.

Remember the most important part of the message? We all stood up for it. It is the gospel. "Gospel" literally means "good news." Our job is to go and tell the good news.

So here's a pop quiz. Who in the world is most in need of good news? That would be people who need good news, of course—people whose lives might not seem filled with good news—people who are hungry, lonely, sick, cold, confined, or unloved. The church, because it is apostolic, has a mission to all the poor and the outcast of the world to make their lives better. Jesus wants the hungry to be fed and the sick to be healed. It's our job to make that happen, even at the cost of self-sacrifice. And in doing these apostolic works, we are sharing our faith in Jesus. Our hope is that those we help will come to the faith we share and, in turn, help others who are in need.

✛ Ten themes of service ✛

Our message of good news falls into ten major themes (called Catholic social teaching). These themes flow from Scripture and the teaching of the church.

1. **All humans have dignity.** Every human being is sacred because we are all made in the image and likeness of God.

2. **We all work for the common good.** We do not exist alone, but in community. Our human dignity can only be fully realized in a community that strives for the good of all.

3. **We all have rights, and we all have responsibilities.** Because we are human, we have rights that flow from our human dignity. Likewise, we have a duty to ensure the dignity of all other humans.

4. **The poor get most of our attention and effort.** Throughout Scripture, God shows a special love for the poor. It is the poor who have their human dignity most threatened. Therefore, if we want to be followers of Jesus, we must be lovers of the poor.

5. **We join with the world to make the world a better place.** Just as we are called to participate in the liturgy, we are called to participate in society. And we also have to work for the equal participation of all groups in society, striving to eliminate racism, sexism, and religious discrimination.

6. **Everyone has a right to a basic, living wage.** People have a right to productive work, fair wages, and economic well being. It is the mission of the church to work for fair economic conditions for everyone.

7. **We work to sustain the resources of the earth.** This goes back to Genesis (the first book of the Bible) where God gave the care of the earth to Adam and Eve. As Christians, we are responsible for the stewardship of the resources of the earth.

8. **All people are one with us.** More so than ever before, we are aware that all the people of the earth are one family. When a child in a far away country goes to bed hungry, we have to feel the pain as though that child were our own child.

9. **We participate in the government to make it fair for everyone.** Government also has a role in ensuring the common good. People of faith are called to interact with the government to help it carry out that responsibility.

10. **We strive to make the world a peaceful place.** Pope John Paul II said, "Peace is not just the absence of war." A central component of the Christian mission is to work for true and lasting peace.

You will, of course, be learning to serve in these ways during your formation period. You don't need to wait until you are baptized to begin serving as a disciple of Christ.

✠ Summary ✠

So these are the four major disciplines of Christian life: worship, word, community, and service.

Worship

We worship God in the official liturgical prayer of the church. That is, in fact, the primary way in which we worship. But the liturgy also inspires us to worship God in our daily lives. So when we thank God for the small blessings during the day, or we praise God for being "in" the thunderstorm, or we contemplate the face of God in the face of a loved one, we are making our whole lives an act of worship.

Word

We already mentioned that the primary job of a catechumen is to hear and reflect on God's word. "Word" itself is a metaphor. God doesn't literally speak to us as I might speak to you on the telephone. When we talk about God's word or God speaking, we are using symbolic language. In the liturgy, we hear God's word primarily in the Scripture readings. But God also speaks to the assembly through the prayers, the songs, the preaching, the symbols, and the actions of the liturgy.

In addition, God "speaks" to the church and guides it throughout history. By discerning God's will, the church has the authority to teach what God "says" to God's people.

And God "speaks" to each of us individually in our hearts as we pray and as we try to live our lives according to God's will.

Community

We also learn to see God in the gathering of people God has called. The people of God is so clearly a reflection of God that we use the same language (metaphor) for the gathering as we do for Jesus—the body of Christ. By gathering as a body of believers—especially for the purpose of worshiping God—we are saying to ourselves and to the world that this community is the clearest thing we have on earth for describing "God." God is a community of love. We show God's love to the world by praying, sharing our faith, remaining hope-filled, believing and acting like God is guiding our steps, and loving others in the world—even at the cost of self-sacrifice.

Service

Sometimes, we can think of serving others—especially the poor—as something we volunteer to do in our spare time. Yet, all the other disciplines of the faith—worship, word, community—should help us to see that serving others is our entire purpose for being. A key turning point for many people is realizing that baptism is not just a ticket into the church or into heaven. It is also your promise to go out and love others—especially the poor—the way Jesus loves them.

When we talk about being Catholic, this is what we mean. Catholics live a life that is focused on worship, word, community, and service. For that reason, your formation process is made up of an apprenticeship in each of those four areas of Catholic living.

- Who do you think of as "poor"? Think of people who are not only financially poor but poor in other ways.

- How do you reach out to the poor in your life?

- Think about the four disciplines of faith that we have been discussing: worship, word, community, and service. Where are you strongest? What do you need to strengthen?

What's expected of you?

WHEN I WAS IN SCHOOL, I always wanted to know what was going to be on the test. Just tell me what I have to learn, and I'll learn it—at least well enough to pass. Of course the "test" for you is a little different. It's the same test for all of us, really. There's only one question. Have we become more like Christ?

If you are a catechumen or a non-practicing baptized person, you will want to pay attention to and imitate the people around you who are living the way of Christ.

If you are an active Christian, seeking full communion with the Catholic Church, you will mostly need to keep doing what you've been doing. You've probably already discovered some of the differences between Catholics and the tradition you were raised in. Generally, though, all Christians are more alike than different.

However, in order to move on to the next stage of your initiation or reception into full communion, the church does have some specific guidelines. I'd like to say that everyone who is leading a formation process in a Catholic parish is aware of these guidelines and is focused on helping newcomers understand and live up to them. Often that is true. But not always. So don't be surprised if no one ever told you this before.

✦ Beginners in faith ✦

Let's start with the beginners. Let's imagine you are not baptized and you have become intrigued with Catholics. In that case, you set the agenda. The expectations the church has of you are those that you set for yourself. If you just want to get a few questions answered, that's fine. If you want to learn a little more about who Catholics are and what we do, we can help you with that. If you'd like some insight into who God is or how to pray, we're the folks who can teach you. It's a little bit like meeting someone you might be interested in dating. At first, you are just getting to know each other. There is no commitment.

✦ Ready for more commitment ✦

Next, let's suppose you'd like to go a step further. Suppose you've been meeting with some Catholics in the parish for some time now and you feel pretty strongly that this is the right thing for you. After lots of conversation and prayer, you decide you'd like to become a Catholic. To continue the dating analogy, after you've been going out a while, you may decide to take things to the next level. At that point, the expectations get a little clearer. Becoming a Catholic is not like joining a club. It's more like joining a team. To become Catholic means you want to become a Christian—a follower of Jesus. A stronger word than "follower" is "disciple." You are saying you want to enter into a discipleship—as in "discipline"—of living as a Christian. If that's really what you want, all the Catholics are going to be stand-on-their-hands-and-do-back-flips overjoyed. However, that joy will be complete when we see you make a true commitment to some entry-level disciplines of Christian life.

Specifically, there are five things the church is looking for before you can formally enter into the process of becoming Catholic:

1. There has to be **some indication that you believe in God**. At this point, you don't have to believe *everything* Catholics be-

lieve about God, or even understand it. But you do have to have a sense that there is a divine Creator who loves you and is actively seeking your love.

2. There has to be **some indication of change in your life**. If you have lived all this time *without* acknowledging God in your life, the church wants to see some new behaviors and attitudes in you that demonstrate a response to your beginning belief in God. You don't need to live like a saint. You just need to show some clear intention to *begin* living a little more like Jesus.

3. The church is also looking for **a change of heart**. It's one thing to change your behavior. It is another to really want to change deep inside of you. Perhaps you are tired of living your old lifestyle. Perhaps you have some regrets. You might think those are things your new Catholic friends don't want to know about. Believe me, we've all been there. There really aren't too many saints in the church. Most of us are world-class sinners. Or we used to be. The key to being a good Catholic isn't being perfect. What is key is being sorry for the mistakes we make and resolving—with God's help—to do better. We call this "conversion."

4. And that leads to prayer. If you are really going to ask for God's help, **you have to know how to pray**. You don't have to be an expert pray-er, but you do have to have the beginnings of a prayer life.

5. If you do ask God for help, God will always help you. And the way God will help you most often is through all those Catholics you've been hanging out with. The next indicator the church is looking for is that **you see that we are, in fact, a *church***. We are a people called by God and committed to serving others. Once you begin to understand that you are asking to join a church, and it's clear you feel at home with Christians who are committed to serving others, you'll be ready to take the next step.

✠ Baptized Christians, living the faith ✠

What if you are not a beginner in faith? If you are someone who has been actively living the Christian faith in another tradition, you probably passed through these five stages long ago. For you, the formation process could be very brief and simple. There isn't a one-size-fits-all preparation. You will have to spend some time in prayer and figure out with your formation team what the best process will be for you. But whatever it is, the basis of it will be living the Christian life as fully as possible. We are expecting only entry-level Christian living for the beginners. For those of us who have had lots of practice, the expectations are higher.

Sponsor

The pastor or the leader of your RCIA group will give you a sponsor. This is a gift given to you by the parish. A sponsor is someone who will accompany you during your formation process. Some communities will let you choose your own sponsor. Honestly, I'm not a big fan of that. If you are really brand new at all this, it isn't likely that you're going to know or recognize the qualities necessary for a good sponsor. But everyone is different, and it is difficult to make a blanket rule that covers all possibilities. If you are a long-time Christian, you may very well know who would make a good sponsor. So if you are in a situation where you are choosing your own sponsor, skip down to the section on godparents to see what qualities you should look for. The traits of a good sponsor and a good godparent are the same.

✠ Becoming a catechumen ✠

For the unbaptized, the next step is to formally enter the order of catechumens. Once you have a sponsor, the parish will schedule a liturgy, called the Rite of Acceptance, in which you will declare your intention to become a Christian. This usually takes place at a Sunday Mass, and there will be many rituals you will see for the first time. If this were a dating relationship, it might be like meeting the family for the first time. You'll probably be a little nervous. Even so, as best you can, try to pay attention to the symbols, gestures, and words of the ritual. Remember that everything in liturgy has a surface meaning and a deeper meaning. Keep looking deeper, and try to find the fullest meaning you can in each part of the liturgy.

In this first public ritual, the unbaptized person becomes a member of the church, specifically a member of the order of catechumens. This liturgy marks the beginning of a specific time of formation called the period of the catechumenate. The first thing most people want to know is, how long does it take? How long will you be a catechumen before you can be baptized?

I wish I could give you a definite answer. But I can't. The answer depends on you. It depends on how long it takes you to learn who Jesus is, how to love him, and how to live in a way that reflects Christ to the world. Understanding *how* to live as a Christian isn't terribly difficult. But actually doing it, putting disciplines into place and practicing a new lifestyle, can sometimes take a while to master.

Again, this is similar to dating. Some people fall in love the first time they set eyes on each other. They don't date very long, and they are soon engaged, and then married. Other people date, break up, get back together, seem like they are *never* going to take the plunge, finally get engaged, and maybe stay that way for years before they get married. It really is different for everybody.

If you are baptized, the process might look similar, but it is really very different. In the liturgy for the unbaptized, there is a deep and significant change in the status of the person. The unbaptized person is not yet a member of the church. As a baptized person, you are already a member of the order of the faithful. Still, your step forward in faith is significant. To celebrate this part of your journey, the parish might schedule a separate, optional liturgy for you, called the Rite of Welcoming, or they may combine it with the liturgy for those who are unbaptized. Some of the rituals may be similar to the liturgy celebrated with the unbaptized, but there is a fundamental difference. You are moving forward on a path you've already been on. The unbaptized are just beginning on that path.

Another symbol—the liturgical year

While we can't say for sure how long the formation process will eventually be, we can say what the minimum is. For the unbaptized, the process will take at least one year. It takes a minimum of a year because your training center is the Sunday liturgy. For Catholics and for some other Christians, Sunday isn't just another day in the week. Each Sunday is one Sunday in a year-long string of Sundays that tells the entire story of Jesus. We celebrate the entire mystery of who Jesus is over the course of one year. In order to completely learn who Jesus is, you have to celebrate that entire course with us.

One thing you'll learn as you are going through the liturgical cycle is that we take three days out of the year, around April, to intensify and focus on the central belief of the Christian faith—the death and resurrection of Jesus. It is at the climax of those three days, the Easter Vigil, that we baptize new initiates. In most cases, that's the only time we baptize adults. So if your "year" starts in September, you might be ready to be baptized the following September. But the church isn't ready. So you would still have to wait some months more for the Easter Vigil to come around again.

On the other hand, you might not be ready in a year. Perhaps you don't think you've mastered the Christian lifestyle by the time of your one-year anniversary of becoming a catechumen. That happens sometimes. Fortunately, this isn't school. No one is going to flunk you or kick you out. I knew someone who was a catechumen for three years before she was initiated. Everyone progresses at their own pace. You can remain a catechumen as long as you need for you to learn how to live the way of Christ.

The Way

So what does living the way of Christ look like? The church has very specific criteria for this also. For the unbaptized, before you became a catechumen, you had to show that you had a beginner's understanding of what living as a Christian was about and that you were beginning to take some steps toward living that way. After participating in the life of the church for one liturgical year, the expectation is that you've now moved to a deeper level of living the Christian way of life. To extend the dating analogy, if you're thinking this might be the person you want to spend the rest of your life with, you would probably have some pretty clear expectations of each other. The church's expectation of the catechumen is that you begin to live the way baptized people live.

If you are baptized, and you haven't been living the Christian way of life, the church will have the same expectations of you. Specifically, the church is looking for these things:

1. **A conversion of mind and heart.** That means more than just a desire to live differently, but actually changing your life, turning toward Jesus, and living in a new way, even if this change is difficult.

2. **An understanding of what the church teaches.** You don't need to be a theology expert, but you should know the basics of what Christians believe.

3. **A loving heart.** We're all loving towards our family and friends, but the church is looking for a little more here. As Christians, we strive to be loving towards everyone, even those who are difficult to love. Even the best Christians fail at this, and no one expects you to be perfect at it. But there should be some sign that you are trying to be more loving.

4. Finally, **you really have to want to be baptized and say so publicly** in a ritual at the start of Lent, call the Rite of Election, and again at the Easter Vigil.

Once all these markers of faith are in place, the pastor or the leader of your formation group will schedule the unbaptized for the Rite of Election. We'll say more about election in the next chapter.

- What changes have taken place in you since you began this process?

- How have your expectations of what it means to be Catholic changed?

- How do you feel about the church's expectations of you? Are these expectations more or less what you expected?

Preparing for baptism

After you have been in the catechumenate for a full liturgical year, you may be ready to move on to the next stage of the process. The next stage is to become a member of the elect. To be "elect" has a similar meaning as someone who is elected to public office. The voters choose someone. In this case, it's not voters who choose you, but Christ. Christ chooses you to be a full member of the body.

In this ritual, the bishop, speaking in the name of Christ and in the name of the church, chooses you as someone who is going to be baptized at the coming Easter Vigil. You are still a member of the order of catechumens, but after this ritual you will have a new title. You will be one of the *elect*—one of the *chosen*.

✠ Deciding if you are ready ✠

Sometime before Lent, you and your sponsor will meet with the director of your initiation process to decide if you will become one of the elect that year. (We'll say more about Lent in just a minute.)

You can't simply say you're ready and choose yourself. But you do have a lot to say about the choice. Officially, the bishop is the one who makes the actual choice. You probably won't meet the bishop until the day of your election, however, so he is relying on the testimony of others in order to make his decision. Those who will testify on your behalf include your sponsor, your catechists, your pastor, and anyone else in the parish who knows you.

Don't let the language of "testimony" throw you. In the ancient church, there was actual testimony before the bishop, much like in a courtroom. And the bishop would decide on the worthiness of the catechumen to join the elect based on that testimony. The church was small enough then that the bishop probably also knew the catechumens personally. In real life today, the "testimony" is usually a conversation among you, your sponsor, and the director of your initiation process. Among you, you will discuss your readiness to move to the next stage based on the criteria we talked about above. Sometimes your pastor might also be involved in the conversation. In some cases, the group (including you) decides that you are not quite ready yet. In that case, you would continue participating in the catechumenate as you have been, growing in your understanding of how to live the way of faith. Before the next Lent, you'd have another conversation about your readiness to become one of the elect.

For many catechumens, one full celebration of the liturgical year is enough to prepare them for election. You won't know everything about Catholicism, and you may feel like a very green beginner. That's okay. You're not expected to know everything to be baptized. You're expected to have learned the basics of what it means to live as a Christian. The sacrament is called "initiation," not "graduation." Your baptism is just the start of learning and growing in faith.

All right, let's say everyone agrees it's time for you to move on to the next step. Before the Rite of Election, you need to select a godparent.

✠ Godparent ✠

Most adults choose only one godparent, but you may choose two people. If you choose two, you have to choose one man and one woman. Many catechumens ask their sponsor to be their godparent. You can certainly do that, but you're not required to. The commitment your sponsor made was to walk with you for the time you were in the catechumenate. A godparent makes a lifetime commitment to you.

Whoever you choose as your godparent, your pastor has to agree with your choice. The things your pastor will look for in a godparent—and the things you should look for too—are these:

- Is the potential godparent a good example of a Catholic?

- Can the person be a good friend to the catechumen?

- Can the person show the catechumen how to live the way of faith?

- Can the person help the catechumen to not feel hesitant or anxious?

- Does the person bear witness to the faith?

- Can the person guide the catechumen's progress in the baptismal life?

✠ The Rite of Election ✠

The choice or election happens in a liturgy, called the Rite of Election, with the bishop and all the other catechumens from the churches in your local area who will be baptized at the upcoming Easter Vigil. This liturgy usually takes place on the First Sunday of Lent at the cathedral. If you've never been to the cathedral, ask your godparent to take you early and show you around. If your godparent has never been to the cathedral, ask a member of the catechumenate team to meet the two of you there and show both of you around.

The Rite of Election might take place within a liturgy of the word or it might take place within a full Mass. If it is Mass, you will be dismissed after the election ritual. Your godparent will remain for Eucharist, and you and the rest of the elect will probably gather with a catechist to reflect on what you experienced in the ritual.

The actual election takes place after the homily. There are four parts, all of which are very simple but very powerful.

1. The godparents and the rest of the community affirm that the catechumens are ready to become elect.

2. The catechumens give their names to the bishop. You will do this by writing your names in the book of the elect. (In some places, the actual writing of names happens before in the parish and the parish book is presented at this point.)

3. The bishop declares the catechumens to be members of the elect.

4. The godparents officially take on their responsibility, and the community prays for the elect.

Before the Rite of Election, you will probably celebrate a ritual in your parish at Sunday Mass in which your community sends you to the cathedral. The sending rite is optional, but most parishes do it. Sometimes in this sending ritual, there is actual testimony about your readiness from your sponsor and your godparent, if that's a different person. Sometimes there might be testimony from other members of the catechumenate team or other parishioners as well.

The Rite of Election is one of the most solemn and profound moments in the life of the church. The introduction to the Rite of Election says this rite "is the focal point of the church's concern for the catechumens" (121). What that means is, from the very first time you met some of the Catholics and started getting to know them, the parish has been praying for you and hoping for this moment. And Catholics around the world are praying for all of the elect at this time—praying for strength and joy as you prepare during this final stage of your initiation.

At the moment you are chosen at the Rite of Election, your time in the period of the catechumenate ends and you start a new, briefer, more intense time of preparation. Some people describe it as similar to getting engaged.

✷ The "already-elect" ✷

If you are baptized, you won't be participating in the Rite of Election because you are *already* chosen. You are already a full member of the body of Christ. Your job is to stand with the rest of the assembly, praying for those who are unbaptized. In some places, there is an optional rite that takes place at the cathedral at the beginning of Lent for all those who are baptized and are participating in the catechumenate process. This is called the "Rite of Calling the Candidates to Continuing Conversion." Sometimes it is combined with the Rite of Election, and sometimes it is celebrated separately. Where I live, it isn't celebrated at all. When it is celebrated, it is a recognition of your ongoing conversion as a baptized person. It is not "election" or choosing. (You were elected at your baptism!)

✷ Lent ✷

The word "Lent" comes from an old Anglo-Saxon word that means "spring." Lent lasts for about forty days, starting with Ash Wednesday and ending before sundown on the Thursday before Easter. Lent is a time of retreat and spiritual preparation for you. But of course, it's impossible to simply go on retreat for the six weeks of Lent. You might have a job (or school) and you might have kids. I'm sure you have a life. But perhaps you could find a way to slow down. Watch less TV. Skip a trip to the mall. Don't take on extra projects at work if you can avoid it. Try especially hard not to do any work on the Sundays of Lent. This is the last time in your life in which you'll be preparing for your baptism. Savor it. Focus on these weeks, and pay attention to how the spirit works in you.

✠ Ash Wednesday ✠

Lent begins on Ash Wednesday—the Wednesday before the election rite. So technically, you will not be a member of the elect on this day. But it would be good to consider this the beginning of your lenten retreat in preparation for your initiation. There are no specific rites for the catechumens on Ash Wednesday. And it is not a holy day of obligation for Catholics. Perhaps because of those reasons, some parishes tend to overlook inviting the catechumens to this liturgy. It is a pretty significant day in the life of most communities, and you should try to be there if at all possible. Ask your sponsor or godparent to take you.

The reason it's called "Ash Wednesday" is because everyone is marked with an ashen cross on their forehead at this liturgy. The ashes symbolize our repentance for our sins and Christ's death on the cross. You or your sponsor might not be sure if it is okay for you to receive ashes since you are not yet baptized. It is okay. A person doesn't have to be baptized to receive ashes. One question new folks (and sometimes lifelong Catholics) have is, is it okay to wash off the ashes after the liturgy? Many people leave the ashes on their foreheads until bedtime. If you go to a liturgy in the morning or afternoon, the ashes can be a silent witness to your faith throughout the day. However, if this is your first Ash Wednesday and you're a little uncomfortable about wearing ashes all day, it's perfectly fine to wash them off.

✠ Fasting ✠

One thing you'll hear a lot about in Lent is fasting. Catholics don't really fast, as in giving up food completely. Instead we cut back on our meals and abstain from certain foods or activities. The idea of fasting or abstaining is to remind us that we are not dependent on earthly goods; we depend only on God.

There are also other reasons for fasting. In the Old Testament, people would fast in preparation for something important, such as a war, or in times of mourning the dead, and as a way of praying in times of distress. In the New Testament, Jesus fasted for forty days in the desert before beginning his ministry. In current times, people might fast if they have a difficult decision to make or if they are about to undertake a momentous task.

When I was a child, every Friday was a "fast" day—in commemoration of the day of the week on which Jesus was crucified. All Catholics were required to refrain from eating meat on Fridays. In the 1960s, the requirement was lifted for all Fridays except for the Fridays of Lent. So in Lent, we don't eat meat on Fridays. And the church still encourages us to refrain from eating meat on the rest of the Fridays of the year, but that's optional. I still try to give up meat every Friday, and you might consider trying it as a spiritual discipline.

There are also three days of the year in which we have a stricter fasting discipline. The rule is that we eat only two light meals (more like snacks) and one regular meal on those days. We are bound by this rule on Ash Wednesday and Good Friday. Then, the church encourages us, especially the elect, to fast on Holy Saturday in preparation for the Easter Vigil and the initiation sacraments. Officially, the fasting rules apply only to those between the ages of twenty-one and fifty-nine, but almost every Catholic abides by them, no matter what age.

In addition to the official fasts, most Catholics have a custom of giving up or at least cutting back on something for Lent. For children, it is often candy, a favorite video game, or cell phone use. For adults, it might be the same. Or it might be something that tempts us beyond reason or that we think we can't live without. Some examples of things adults often give up during Lent include drinking, swearing, shopping, meat (every day of Lent), and working late. You can ask your sponsor or godparent and other Catholics you know what they are giving up to give you more ideas.

Two kinds of fasting

The fasting of Lent and abstaining from meat on the Fridays of the year are considered penitential fasts. This fasting helps us remember we are often tempted by things that are not good for us. The fasting of Good Friday and Holy Saturday is considered a preparatory fast. It is meant to help the elect focus on prayer and getting ready for the big event of the Easter Vigil.

Eucharistic fast

There is another preparatory fast that all Catholics are obligated to make. Any time we share in Communion at Mass, we are required to abstain from all food and drink for at least one hour before the time we receive the Body and Blood of Christ. This rule, of course, will not apply to you until after your baptism because you are not yet coming to the eucharistic table.

✠ Scrutinies ✠

Part of your commitment as a catechumen is to celebrate liturgy with the community every Sunday. But it's possible you missed a few Sundays here and there throughout your formation year. I'm sure you had a very good reason, and no, you don't need a note from your mother. But you really need to try extra hard to be at church every Sunday of Lent, especially if you are member of the elect. And you cannot, must not, dare not miss three particular Sundays—the scrutiny Sundays. Even if it is still early in your formation year, you should find out from your initiation director when the scrutinies are and mark them on your calendar now. Don't plan any out-of-town trips on those days. According to the church, only the bishop can excuse one of the elect for being absent from any of the scrutinies.

Don't get too freaked out by the word "scrutiny." No one is going to be grilling you or trying to get you to reveal some deep secret. These are spiritual scrutinies that are ritual prayers for your preparation for initiation. The purpose of the scrutinies is twofold. First, it is a prayer that is meant to bring out and strengthen all the strong and good aspects of your faith. Second, it is a prayer to protect you from temptation and give you the strength you need to overcome any weakness or hesitation you might feel as you move closer to baptism. It is a series of three rituals, and the effect of the prayer is supposed to build over the three weeks. The rituals are simple, but very powerful. This is an essential part of your preparation for baptism.

The scrutinies are only for the unbaptized. The baptized candidates participate with the rest of the assembly and are not intended to be the subjects of this ritual since it is a preparation for baptism.

✢ Passion (Palm) Sunday ✢

Passion Sunday is the final Sunday of Lent and begins Holy Week. There are no specific rituals for the elect on this day, but it is an important day in your preparation. On this day, we hear the story of Jesus' suffering and death. Way back at the Rite of Acceptance, when you said yes to following the cross, this is what you said yes to. Jesus gives up everything, including his life, for our sakes. When we agree to follow the cross, we are agreeing to do the same as Jesus did. So, just before your baptism, it is important to be reminded of the path you chose.

✢ Triduum ✢

Holy Thursday

Lent ends on the Thursday before Easter. We call this day "Holy Thursday." At sundown on Holy Thursday, the Easter Triduum begins with the Mass of the Lord's Supper. "Triduum" means three days. Over the next three days (counted from sundown Thursday to sundown Sunday), the church celebrates one really long liturgy. We break it up so we are not in church for the entire time. But once the Mass starts on Thursday, you can think of yourself as being "at liturgy" until sundown on Easter Sunday. A distinctive element of the Holy Thursday liturgy is the washing of the feet. The way the washing happens varies from parish to parish. In every case, though, no matter how it is celebrated, it is intended to remind us that Jesus washed the feet of his disciples. We are called to serve others in the same way as Jesus, humbling ourselves before their needs.

Good Friday

All of Good Friday is a day of prayer. Years ago, most businesses would be closed on this day (the New York Stock Exchange still is). Even if a business wasn't closed, the Catholics that worked there would take the day off. If you aren't able to take Good Friday off, try at least to take short breaks for prayer throughout the day. The official prayer of the day is the reading of the Passion of Jesus and the veneration of the cross. If the service times at your parish conflict with your work schedule, find a church nearby your workplace that might have a service you can get to over your lunch hour.

You might wonder why we are reading the Passion (the story of Jesus' crucifixion) again, when we just read it on Passion Sunday. The account we read on Passion Sunday is chosen from among the gospels of Matthew, Mark, or Luke. The Passion we hear on Good Friday is always from the Gospel of John. Passion Sunday is the last Sunday of Lent, and the versions of the Passion in Matthew, Mark, and Luke focus more on the aspects of Jesus being abandoned by his followers (and even by God) and on elements of forgiveness. The account in John, which is read during the Easter Triduum, is more about God's victory over death and focuses on the moment of crucifixion as the ultimate revelation of Jesus as the Son of God. If you read each account side by side, you'll immediately see the differences in tone.

While the four gospels are different, Jesus is not. There was only one Jesus. However, the four writers each have a different understanding of the most important parts of Jesus' story that needs to be told. In order to get the full picture, we need to hear from each one of them.

Holy Saturday

Okay, we already said all of Lent is a retreat. Lent ends with the Mass of the Lord's Supper on Holy Thursday, and we begin the three days of the Triduum. In the middle of those three days is Holy Saturday. There are no major liturgical services on Holy Saturday until the Easter Vigil, which begins after sundown. The day itself is meant to be an even more intense retreat than Lent. It is a day of preparation for your initiation at the Vigil. Plan ahead to take this day off. No working. No shopping. No cleaning. No cooking if there is someone else who can do it. Your job today is to pray, just as Jesus did in the garden before his crucifixion. No, you're not going to be crucified. But you are going to "die" to your old way of life by being "buried" in the waters of baptism. So spend some concentrated time on this day focusing on your journey so far and where you are being called to go.

There are some simple rituals that might be celebrated during the day on Holy Saturday. The first possibility is the recitation of the Creed. If you were officially presented with the Creed during your catechumenate period or during Lent, this is the ritual in which you and the other elect recite it back for the community.

Another possible ritual is the Ephphetha (EHF-uh-thuh) Rite. *Ephphetha* is a Greek word that means "be opened." The ritual is a simple prayer that your lips will be opened so you will be able to profess your new faith and give praise to God.

In some countries, it is also possible to celebrate a ritual for choosing a baptismal name. We don't celebrate that ritual in the United States. People are baptized by their given name. However, some communities do adapt the ritual to honor the given names of all those to be baptized.

✝ Baptized candidates ✝

I sometimes hear that baptized candidates feel left out during Lent and the Triduum because so much of the focus is on the unbaptized. I think I understand why this happens, and I'd like ask those of you who are baptized to stretch your thinking a little. When you first approached someone in the parish, you probably expressed an interest in "becoming Catholic." The unbaptized probably said something similar. But, as we discussed earlier, those who are baptized—even if they've never been to church since the day of their baptism—are fundamentally different from the unbaptized. The unbaptized aren't becoming "Catholic" so much as they are becoming "Christian."

For someone from another Christian tradition to become Catholic is usually a very big step. It might seem like the biggest step of your life. But as big as it is, it is not the same transformation that took place at your own baptism when you became a member of the body of Christ.

I think of it like two children born in a foreign country—let's call them Peter and Pierre, born in France. Peter's parents are United States citizens, and Pierre's parents are not. The two children grow up together as best friends and are completely "French" in every way. One day, they decide to move to the United States. The minute they step off the plane at JFK, Peter has a whole host of privileges and rights that Pierre does not. It doesn't matter that Peter is unaware of these rights, knows nothing of U.S. history, and cannot even speak English. He is a full and complete U.S. citizen.

It is similar with some baptized candidates who are becoming Catholic. You may not be aware of all the gifts you were given at your baptism, and you may not speak "Catholic" very well. Nevertheless, you are an integral member of the body of Christ—a member of the order of the faithful.

So, even though all this feels brand new, your role during Lent and Triduum is to participate *with* the baptized Catholics in welcoming and initiating the elect into the way of faith.

For the baptized, both those seeking to be received into full communion with the Catholic Church and those who are already Catholic, the way we enter into Lent is to focus on living out our baptism more faithfully. We recall and recommit ourselves to the four disciplines the catechumens are only just now learning—worship, word, community, and service. In this way, we reclaim and renew our baptism, and we become more like Christ. At the same time, our renewal of our own baptism provides example and support to the catechumens as they look forward to joining us in the order of the faithful.

- What do you see as the biggest difference between being a catechumen and being a member of the elect?

- What are you most looking forward to about the day of your baptism? Or what are you most looking forward to about the day of your reception into full communion with the Catholic Church?

- After coming this far on the journey, describe what you now think it means to be Catholic.

Your baptism

Your baptism is going to be a very big deal. Or, if you are already baptized, your baptism still is a very big deal. Remember earlier we talked about the liturgical year being a symbol? The crown jewel of that symbol is "Easter." If you are new to church language, you might think of Easter as the one Sunday of the year when the President hosts an egg hunt on the White House lawn. What Catholics mean by Easter is a fifty-day festival of faith.

Okay, some of us Catholics think of the one-day-a-year-egg-hunt thing too, but we are *supposed* to be thinking of the fifty days. Those fifty days are measured Sunday to Sunday over eight Sundays, starting on Easter Sunday. Every one of the eight Sundays is just like Easter Sunday—a great festival.

These eight Sundays are the most important Sundays of the year, especially if you were just baptized or just recently received into full communion with us. It is especially important that you are at Mass on each of these Sundays, because it is in the Masses of the Easter season where we reflect on and celebrate the full impact of your baptism. In some parishes, the newly baptized even wear the white robe they received at baptism to Mass for each of these eight Sundays.

For those of you who will be newly baptized, Easter will be the first time when you will regularly gather with the rest of the faithful at the Lord's Table for Eucharist.

For the baptized candidates, you may have been received into full communion some months earlier or only recently. But no matter when you joined us in full communion, your first Easter season as a Catholic is also an important time to reflect on and celebrate your baptism.

✢ Welcome to the big leagues ✢

There is a 1988 baseball movie, *Bull Durham*, about a veteran catcher who is sent to a minor league team to teach a hotshot rookie how to pitch like a major league player. The catcher has a "creed" that he lives by in the "church of baseball," and he is frustrated through much of the movie because the rookie seems to have no true belief of his own. In the end, though, the rookie learns how to play—and believe—at a new level and goes on to play for a major league team.

The analogy limps a little because being a Christian has nothing to do with how fast you can throw a baseball. But there does come a time when you are a full member of the team—a member of the body of Christ. As a "rookie," you may still have a lot to learn. But you are also expected to pull your weight, to make your contribution.

The analogy, weak as it might be, works on this level. Christianity, like baseball, is a discipline. You have to get up every day and practice your faith. In baseball, players practice the "fundamentals." For Christians, the fundamentals are the four areas we discussed earlier: word, community, worship, and service. If you follow the way of faith in each of those four disciplines every day of your life, you will grow stronger and stronger as a member of the body of Christ.

You will also get discouraged. The church won't turn out to be as wonderful as you imagined it would. Your fellow Christians will not always live up to the ideals you have become so committed to. Your life may not become immediately better. These times of discouragement happen to all of us. It is exactly at these moments that you need to rely on your faith and on your brothers and sisters in Christ (flawed as we may be). No one of us is strong enough to carry the entire burden of the mission Christ left us. But Jesus promised us that together, as the body of Christ, our burden will be light. We will all be counting on you—just as much as you will be counting on us.

God bless you on your journey.

APPENDICES

Postures for prayer

When Catholics pray, we use a lot of different postures. It isn't possible to come up with one single meaning for each posture, but people will try. Some will say that posture X is more respectful than posture Y. Other will say posture A is more traditional that posture B. Here's a general rule of thumb. When you are praying alone, whatever posture helps you feel closest to God is the posture you should use. I sit. I have a friend who prays while jogging. Some people kneel. I read somewhere that Pope John Paul II would lie prostrate on the floor. Whatever works for you is what you should do.

But when you are praying in community, that's a different story. You should see yourself as a member of a unified body. If everybody is standing, you should stand, for example. At Sunday Mass, there are designated postures for the different parts of the liturgy, but not every parish does them the same way. Your sponsor will help you know when to sit, stand, and kneel. Ideally, everyone should be sharing the same postures throughout the liturgy. When we all share a common posture, we are showing that we are all one body.

Knowing that we cannot say everything about each posture, here are some things to think about.

Standing

Standing is the most ancient of public prayer postures, dating back to our Jewish roots. This posture is most often used for prayers of thanksgiving, praise, and blessing.

Kneeling

Kneeling is usually associated with repentance. In 325 AD, the Council of Nicea forbade kneeling at Sunday liturgy because they did not think there was a place for penitence at Mass. Over time, in the Western church, kneeling also came to mean humility and submission. So kneeling came back into the Mass in some places to show our humility before God.

Prostrating

Lying flat on your stomach on the floor is a sign of super-repentance or begging. In the Western church, the only time you are likely to see prostration is on Good Friday. On this day, the presider (and only he and the deacon) lies prostrate before the altar. If you witness an ordination, you will also see prostration. For private prayer, many people lie in bed, either on their back or their stomach.

Sitting

Churches didn't have pews until the middle ages. As we saw, standing was the prayer posture for Mass from early on, so there was no need for pews. Now, sitting is perhaps the most common prayer posture for Western Christians. When you pray in your catechetical sessions, the group is most likely sitting. Sitting is also the traditional posture for the bishop when he teaches or delivers a homily.

Catholic customs

There are hundreds of things Catholics do that are reflections of our Catholic culture. Some are steeped in tradition and meaning, and some seem to have just always existed without any real explanation. I've been Catholic all my life, and I still run across some custom that I never heard of. Customs vary from country to country and among different ethnic groups. These are some of the most common.

✠ Liturgical colors ✠

Colors have long been associated with different feasts or seasons within the church year. The color scheme has varied over time and from place to place. This is the current list of official colors in the United States and their associations. You will see these colors in the vestments worn by the priest and deacon and perhaps in other liturgical elements around the church, such as the altar cloth or the banners.

> **White:** Christmas season, Easter season, feasts of the Lord, Mary, the angels, and saints who were not martyrs, baptisms, weddings, funerals, ordinations
>
> **Green:** Ordinary time
>
> **Red:** Feasts of the Lord's passion, feasts of the martyrs, Palm Sunday, Good Friday, Pentecost, and any feast associated with the Holy Spirit, confirmations
>
> **Violet:** Advent, Lent, and reconciliation liturgies
>
> **Rose** (optional): Third Sunday of Advent, Fourth Sunday of Lent

Black *(optional)*: All Souls Day, funerals

Gold: Gold is not an official color, but some parishes use it in place of or in addition to white on Christmas and Easter

✦ Sign of the cross ✦

When you became a catechumen, the presider and your sponsor made the sign of the cross on you. If you've been going to Mass, you've been crossing yourself. Every liturgy begins with the sign of the cross. Catholics also begin most of our other prayers with the sign of the cross—for example, before meals, before bed, or praying for a loved one who is ill or needs support. When I was in grade school, Sister Paul Mary taught me to make the sign of the cross every time I heard a siren as a silent prayer for whoever is in need. In the Mass, you might have noticed that just before the gospel, some people make a triple sign of the cross with their thumb on their forehead, lips, and breast. This is a prayer that the gospel will be in our minds, on our lips, and in our hearts.

✦ Holy water ✦

Another way we use the sign of the cross is to bless ourselves with holy water. Most churches have small dishes of blessed water at the entrances or the baptismal font at the main entrance. As we enter, we dip our fingers in the holy water and cross ourselves as a remembrance of our baptism. Since you are not yet baptized, you could forgo that ritual if you want. Or you could bless yourself as a foretaste of the baptism you are preparing for.

In the liturgy, sometimes there is a sprinkling rite at the beginning of the liturgy. We are sprinkled with blessed water for the same reason we blessed ourselves coming into church—as a reminder of baptism. Some people take holy water home with them to bless family members and ritual objects.

Holy water is also used in the funeral rites to bless the casket as one final reminder of baptism.

✠ Genuflecting ✠

A genuflection is like an aerobic exercise. You go down on your right knee, touching your knee to the floor, and then stand again. Some people who have bad knees (or are a little lazy) do sort of a half genuflection, half curtsey. A genuflection is a sign of respect and adoration for the Blessed Sacrament reserved in the tabernacle. If the tabernacle is in the altar-area of the church, you would genuflect toward the tabernacle just before entering your pew. In some churches, the tabernacle is in a special chapel. In that case, a genuflection is not necessary in the main area of the church, but many Catholics do it out of habit.

✠ Bowing ✠

A bow is another aerobic exercise that is also a sign of respect and adoration. In the liturgy, we bow to the altar and to the cross. We bow during the Creed when we proclaim the Incarnation ("…by the Holy Spirit was incarnate of the Virgin Mary and became man.") We bow just before sharing in communion. Although not many people do it, it is traditional to bow when singing or saying the names of the persons of the Trinity (Father, Son, and Spirit).

✴ Holy cards ✴

Holy cards aren't as popular today as they were when I was a child. We would joke about them being Catholic baseball cards. A holy card is a small card with a picture of a saint on one side and the story of that saint's life on the back. Sometimes they are used to commemorate a baptism, confirmation, funeral, or other religious anniversary.

✴ Relics ✴

A relic is a personal object associated with a saint. You can't get more personal than your person, so many relics are bone chips or even body parts from the departed. Christianity is filled with tales of miracles attributed to prayer before the relics of saints. The veneration of relics began in the early church by honoring the grave of a saint—the same way we honor the burial sites of loved ones today. Over time, bone chips or pieces of a saint's clothing were shared with other communities so Christians who lived far from the grave could venerate the saint also. Years ago, every church altar used to have a relic embedded in a stone placed within the altar. That's no longer the case, so your parish may or may not have an altar stone, depending on when the church was built.

✴ Eucharistic adoration ✴

Eucharistic adoration is the practice of praying before the Blessed Sacrament (the consecrated bread), housed either in the tabernacle or in a gilded stand called a monstrance. This is a sign of devotion to and worship of Jesus, whom we believe is really present in the consecrated bread. The type of prayer you pray before the Blessed Sacrament is up to you. Many Catholics do what is called "making a visit" to the Blessed Sacrament. They go to church when nothing else is going on and sit or kneel in front of the tabernacle in silent prayer. Some traditions credit St. Francis of Assisi (d. 1226) with having started the practice.

✠ Kissing ✠

Saint Paul writes frequently about greeting fellow Christians with a holy kiss (for example, 1 Corinthians 16:20). The practice carried over into the liturgy as the sign of peace. Today, we have replaced the kiss with a handshake. However, there is still a lot of kissing in the liturgy. At the beginning and end of Mass, the priest kisses the altar. The deacon or priest kisses the gospel after proclaiming it. On Good Friday, the assembly processes to the cross to venerate it with either a touch or a kiss. In these cases, the kiss is a sign of reverence. If you are present at an ordination, you will see the ordained offering a "fraternal kiss" to the newly ordained, which is a sign of welcome and unity. Like the kiss of peace at Mass, this fraternal kiss is usually just a hug and a handshake.

✠ Votive candles ✠

Catholics have a tradition of "lighting a candle for someone." It is a physical way to offer a prayer for another person. Often, we are praying for a loved one who has died. In most Catholic churches, there is a stand filled with votive candles. Usually there is a donation box for money to defer the cost of the candles.

For a more complete list of customs, see *Catholic Customs and Traditions: A Popular Guide* by Greg Dues (Twenty-Third Publications).

Annulments

The rules surrounding marriage and annulments can be one of the most confusing aspects of becoming Catholic. People who were married and divorced before they even thought of becoming Catholic often wonder why the church would have anything to say about their former marriage. Here's why.

The church believes in marriage. More importantly, the church believes that the promise a husband and wife make to each other is sacred and eternal. It doesn't matter if you made that promise in a Catholic church, and it doesn't even matter if you were Christian when you made the promise. The church believes God was present at your wedding and in your promise, even if you, yourself, didn't believe it at the time. So, according to the teaching of the church, if you made a solemn vow before God, the church has to honor that vow—even if you are now divorced.

An annulment is not a divorce. A divorce is a dissolution of a marriage. In the eyes of the church, if two people are validly married, that marriage cannot be dissolved. An annulment is a process of discernment to try and understand if the promise you made was an actual, valid promise. For instance, if your former spouse lied to you about some important part of his or her life, you made a promise under false pretenses. Or if you were too immature or didn't understand the nature of your promise, it isn't really a promise. An annulment is granted if the church discerns that the promise of marriage you made couldn't have been made authentically because of circumstances at the time of your marriage. An annulment is a declaration that your marriage vow was never a true vow in the first place.

What about the children?

Some people think that if their marriage is annulled, that means their children are "illegitimate." That's not true. All children are legitimate. The church makes no judgment about the status of your children. An annulment is only about the promise made between spouses, not about their children.

Do I have to get an annulment?

Every situation is different, and you need to talk with your pastor or initiation team leader to find out if you actually need an annulment. If you are divorced and not remarried, you do not need an annulment. However, if you ever decide to get married in the future, you will need one.

If you do need an annulment, and if you are unbaptized, usually you cannot celebrate the rite of election until your annulment is finalized. If you are already baptized and you need an annulment, you cannot be received into full communion until after your annulment is finalized.

What is the process for an annulment?

If you need an annulment, you would first ask to be heard by the church. (This is a formal, written request that a parish minister will assist with.) The parish minister sends all the necessary information to a diocesan office called the tribunal.

The tribunal considers your request and, in the end, returns an answer stating that your marriage is considered either valid or null by the church.

As part of the process, the tribunal will contact your former spouse if possible. The former spouse has a right to participate in the process if he or she wishes. Some cases also require information from witnesses to the marriage. Your parish minister can explain more about the details of this.

The time for the entire process varies from case to case, but it is usually about one year. (It could take longer.)

There is a fee for the process that covers administrative costs and salaries. The fee varies from diocese to diocese. (The average cost is $500; check with your parish minister.) However, no one is ever denied access to the annulment process because they cannot afford the fee.

Excerpted from *The Way of Faith: A Field Guide for the RCIA Process* by Nick Wagner (Twenty-Third Publications).

Outline of the Mass

The Introductory Rites

- Gathering song
- Sign of the Cross and Greeting
- Penitential Act (or Rite of Blessing & Sprinkling)
- Kyrie (Lord, have mercy)
- Gloria (Glory to God)
- Collect (Opening Prayer)

Part I

The Liturgy of the Word

- First Reading
- Responsorial Psalm
- Second Reading
- Gospel Acclamation (Alleluia)
- Gospel Reading
- Homily
- (Dismissal of Catechumens)

- Profession of Faith (Creed)
- General Intercessions (Prayer of the Faithful)

Part II

The Liturgy of the Eucharist

- Preparation of the Gifts
- Eucharistic Prayer
- Communion Rite
  - The Lord's Prayer
  - Sign of Peace
  - Breaking of the Bread
  - Communion
  - Prayer after Communion

The Concluding Rites

- Blessing
- Dismissal